Carom Billiards: Interesting Table Patterns

3-Cushion Billiards Championship Shots

From International Competitions
(Test Yourself against Professional Players)

Allan P. Sand
PBIA Certified Instructor

ISBN 978-1-62505-232-2
PRINT 7x10

ISBN 978-1-62505-421-0
PRINT 8.5x11

First edition

Published by Billiard Gods Productions.
Santa Clara, CA 95051
U.S.A.

For the latest information about books and videos, go to: http://www.billiardgods.com

Acknowledgements

Wei Chao created the software that was used to create these graphics.

Table of Contents

Other books by the author …

      3 Cushion Billiards Championship Shots (a series)

      Carom Billiards: Some Riddles & Puzzles

      Carom Billiards: MORE Riddles & Puzzles

      Why Pool Hustlers Win

      Table Map Library

      Safety Toolbox

      Cue Ball Control Cheat Sheets

      Advanced Cue Ball Control Self-Testing Program

      Drills & Exercises for Pool & Pocket Billiards

      The Art of War versus The Art of Pool

      The Psychology of Losing – Tricks, Traps & Sharks

      The Art of Team Coaching

      The Art of Personal Competition

      The Art of Politics & Campaigning

      The Art of Marketing & Promotion

      Kitchen God's Guide for Single Guys

Introduction

This is one of a series of Carom Billiards books that show how professional players select shots, based on the table layout. All of these shots have been mapped out based on shots played at international competitions.

This book contains a wide variety of interesting shots. They are extraordinary because of how the patterns were played.. These are fun shots, well worth the study and practice.

These shots put you inside the head of the player beginning with the ball positions (shown in the first table layout). The second table layout shows the shooting decision and the results of the player's choice.

About the Graphic Layouts

There are two graphics for each shot. The first graphic shows the ball positions on the table. The ball labeled "A" is always the player's CB. The first graphic the ball positions on the table. The second graphic shows how the shot was played.

Each table graphic in this book is a black & white representation of a standard 5 x 10 carom billiards table. Balls are represented with these three symbols.

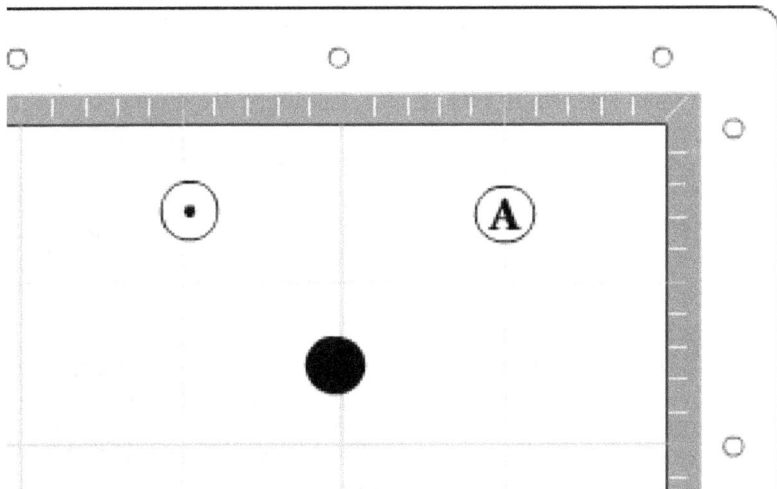

(A) The white "A" ball "A" is ALWAYS the shooter's cue ball.

(•) The white "center dot" ball is always the opponent's cue ball.

● This is the red Object Ball, represented in the layouts as the black ball.

Each shot is represented with two layouts on each page. The first layout shows the ball position setup BEFORE the shot. The second layout shows the ball pathways that the balls travel during the shot.

Table Setup

1. Use donuts (paper reinforcement rings) to mark positions for the carom balls. These are available at any office supply store.

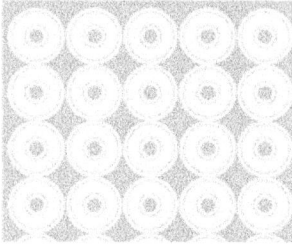

2. Place chalk cubes at the locations where the CB contacts each rail.

When you play the shot, observe where the CB pattern and each rail contact. You may need several attempts as you make adjustments to the CB spin to properly follow the pattern.

Purpose of the Layouts

These are examples of shots that champion 3-cushion players from all over the world had to play. The first graphic provides the layout. The second graphic provides the results of their shooting solution. These layouts are provided for two purposes.

- Use the first layout as a mental exercise. The player picked one, but there are many possibilities. From the comfort of your armchair, you can consider multiple options, and work out the pattern using the spin and speed you would have applied. These help stretch and extend your skills in tactical analysis. Then consider how the player decided how to shoot the shot. From the patterns you can determine how the CB was played and the type of applied spin. It's helpful to use a pointer (or your finger) to trace the pattern as you work out how the shot was played.

- The second purpose is to take these layouts to the practice table. Position the paper reinforcement rings in place for each ball. You are going to shoot the layout many times, so these donuts help mark the ball positions for each attempt. BEFORE you experiment with your own "solutions", shoot the pattern until you can easily duplicate the paths. This means you will do a lot of experimentation to find the spin/speed used by the original player. Only AFTER you understand and can execute the pattern should you experiment with your own ideas.

This combination of mental analysis and practical table practice will boost your growth as an intelligent and thinking carom billiards player.

A: Cushion First

These are interesting shots where the CB first goes into a rail and then completes the necessary contacts with the OBs and other rails.

A: Group 1

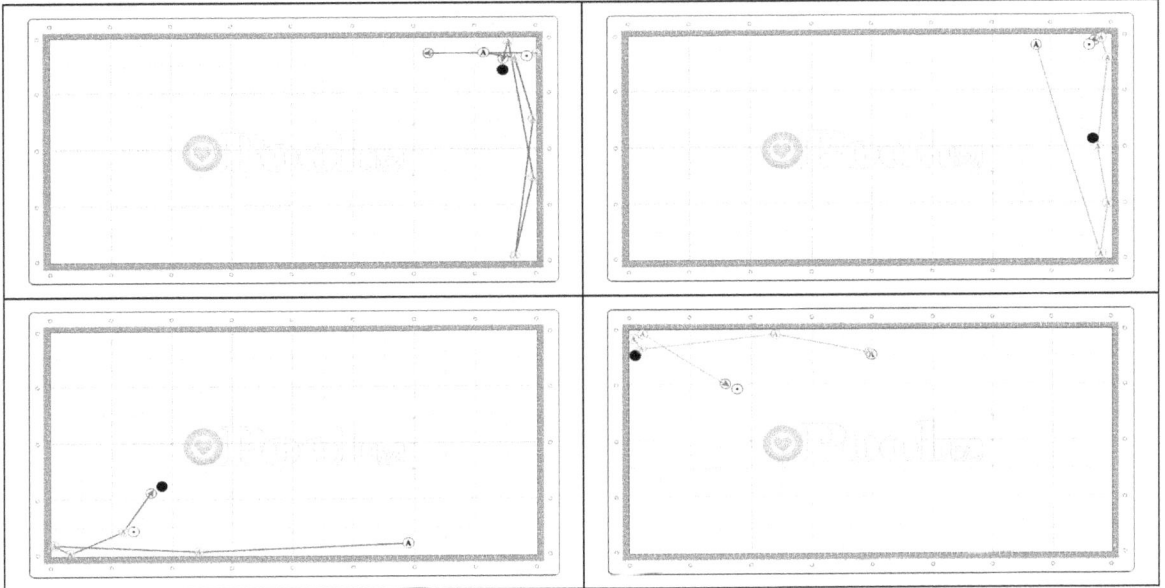

Analysis:

A:1a. _____

A:1b. _____

A:1c. _____

A:1d. _____

A:1a – Setup

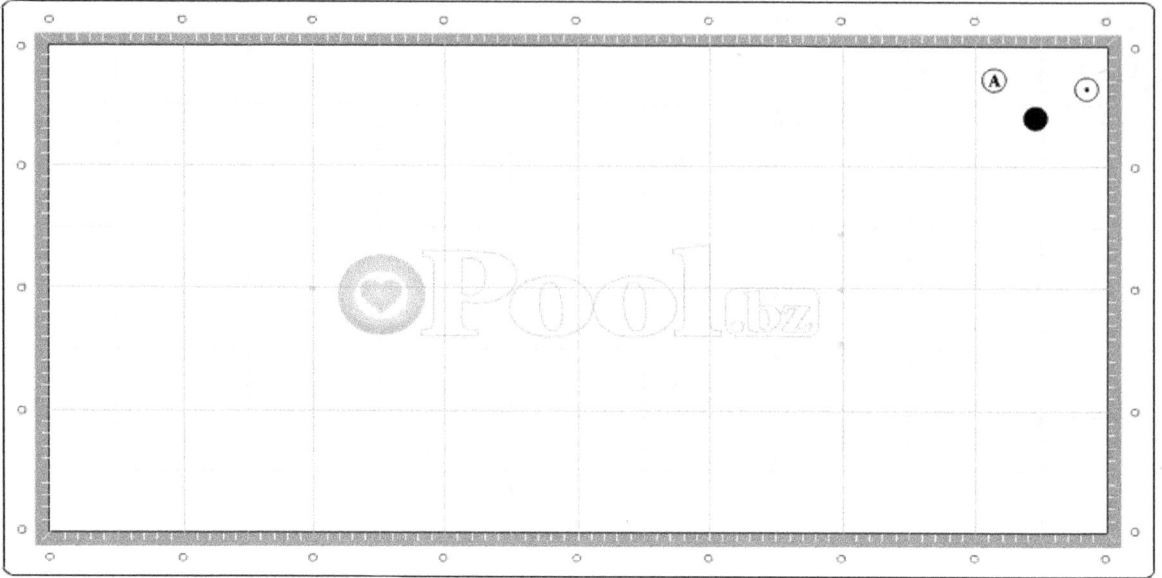

Shot Pattern

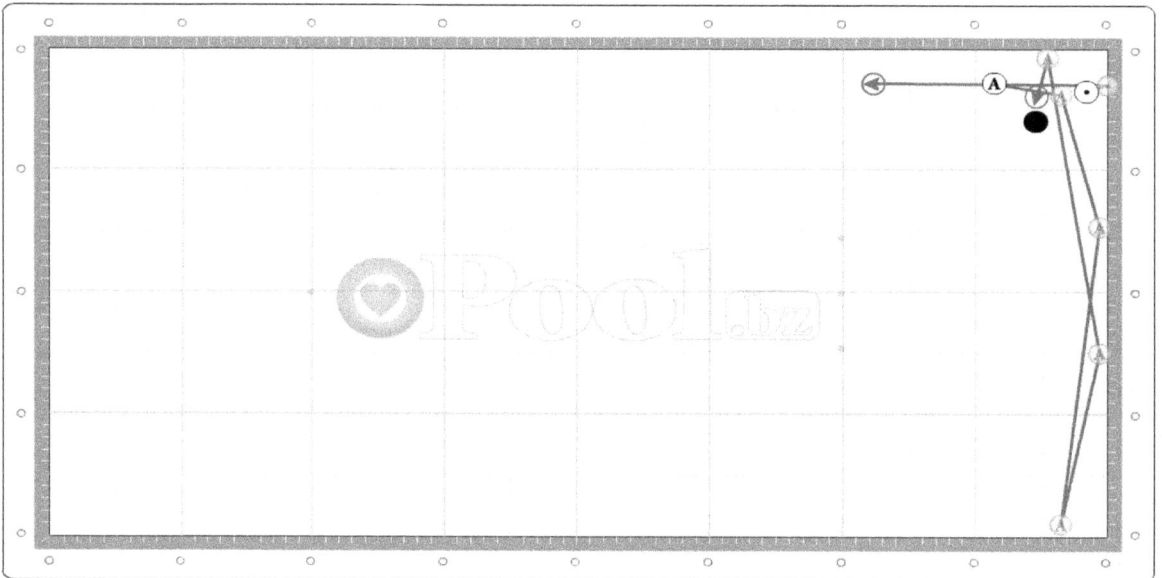

A:1b – Setup

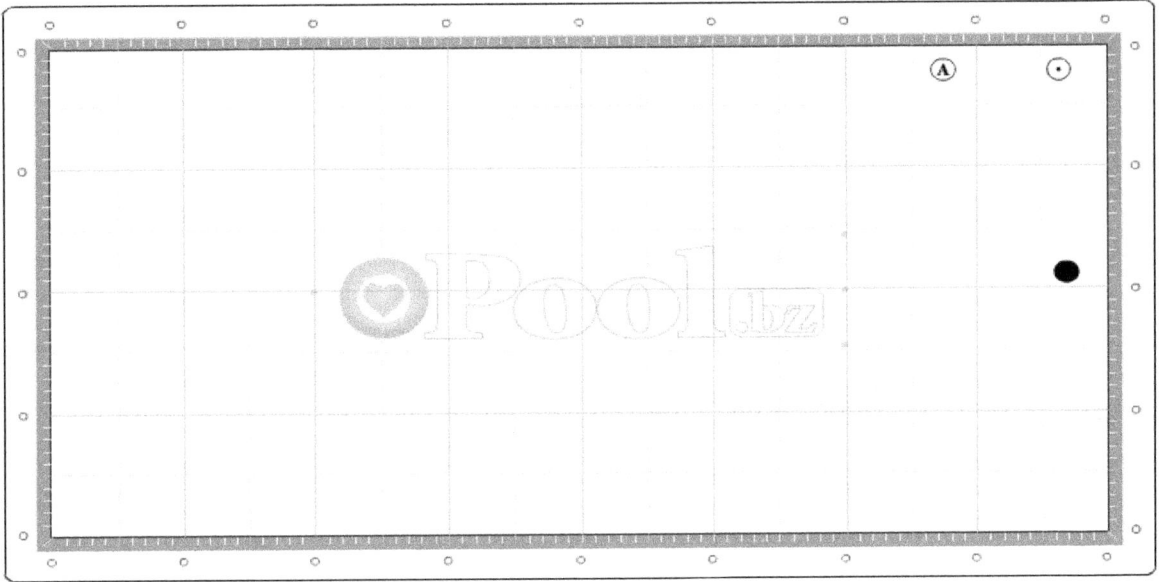

Shot Pattern

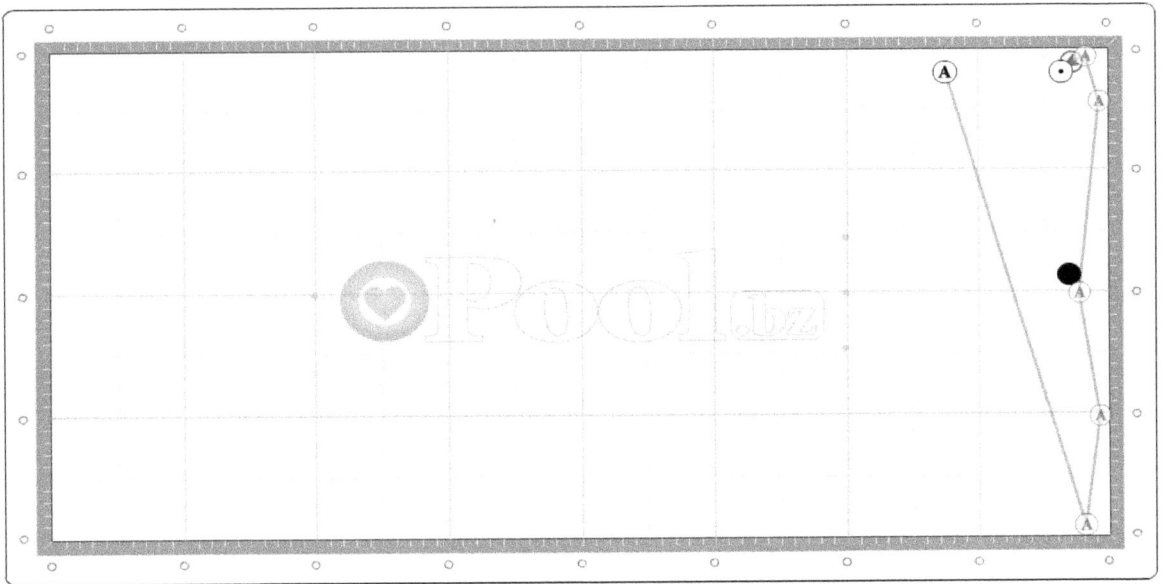

A:1c – Setup

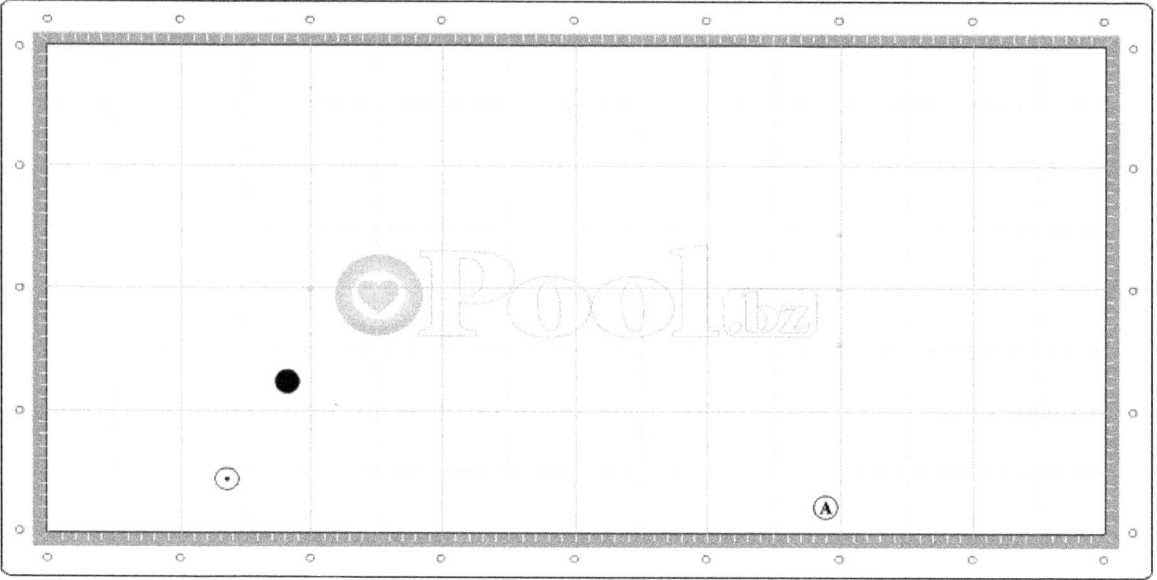

Shot Pattern

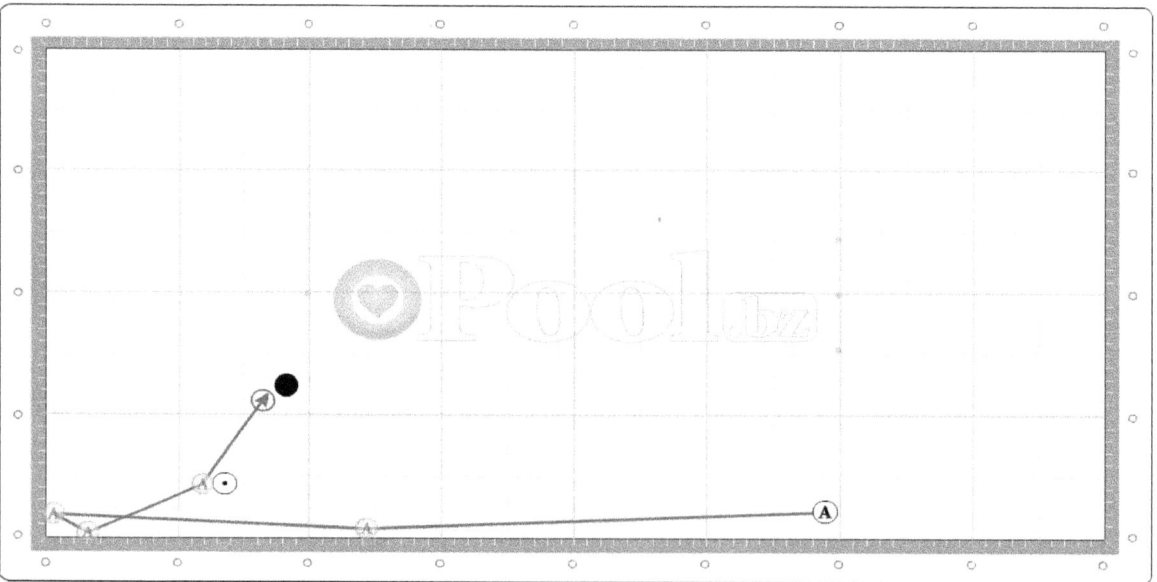

A:1d – Setup

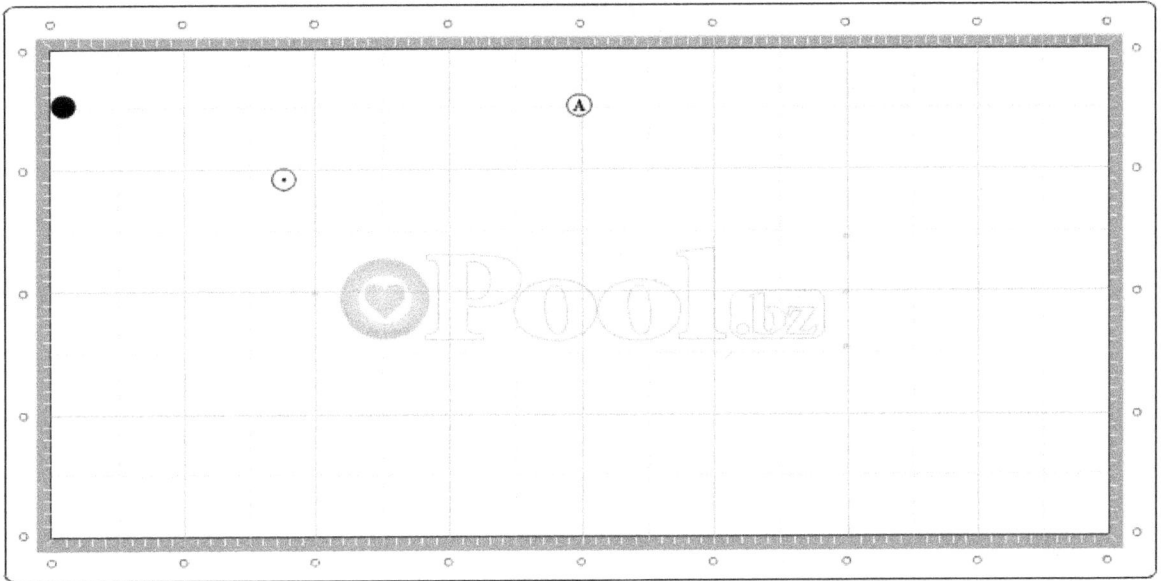

Shot Pattern

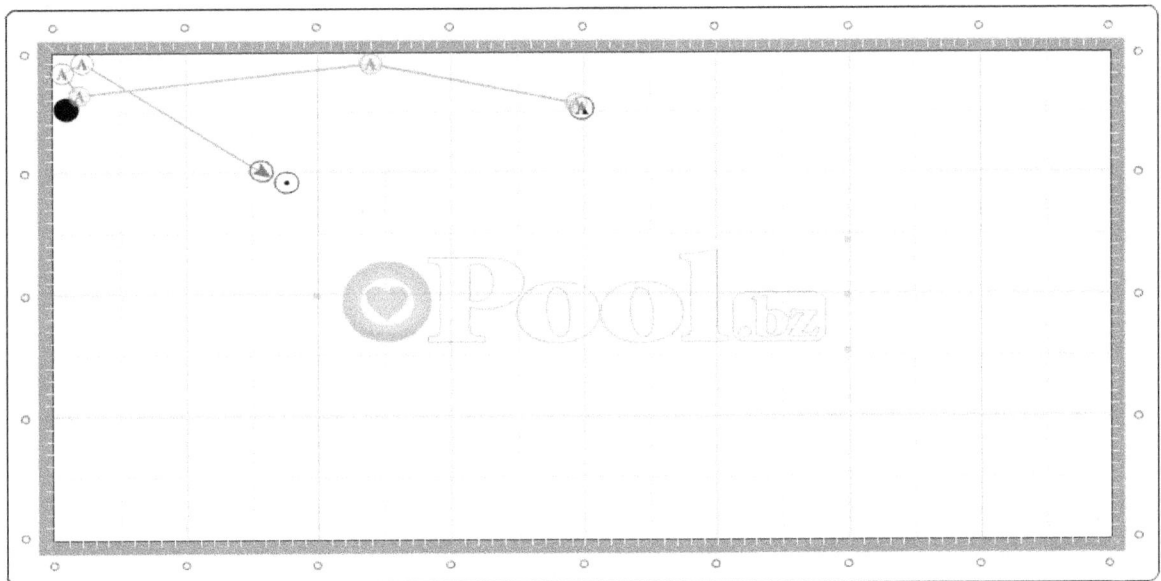

A: Group 2

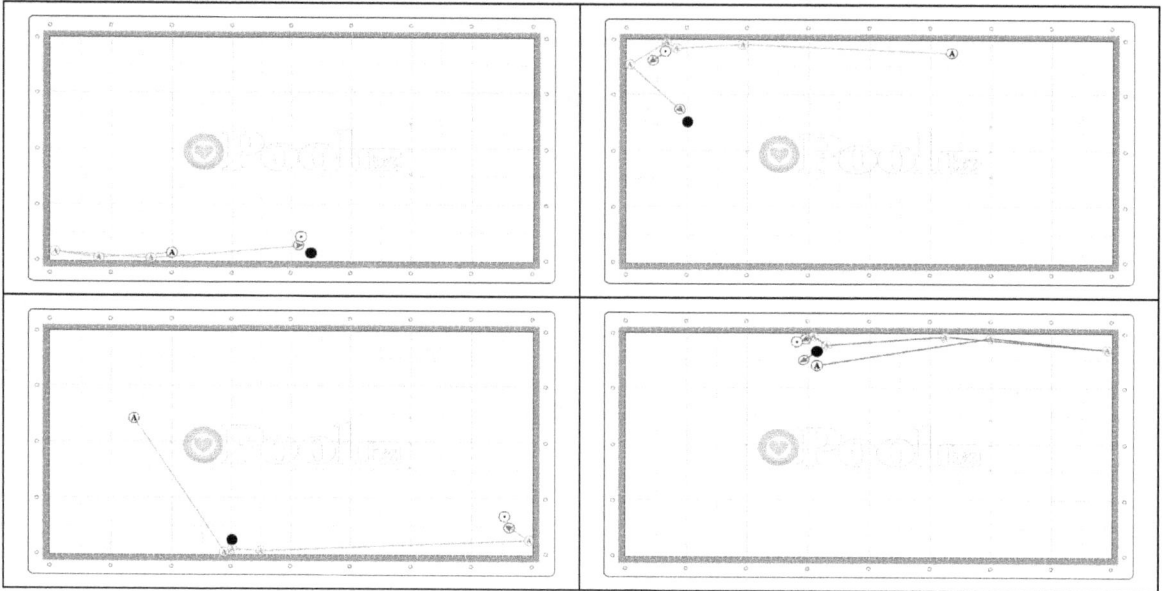

Analysis:

A:2a. _____

A:2b. _____

A:2c. _____

A:2d. _____

A:2a – Setup

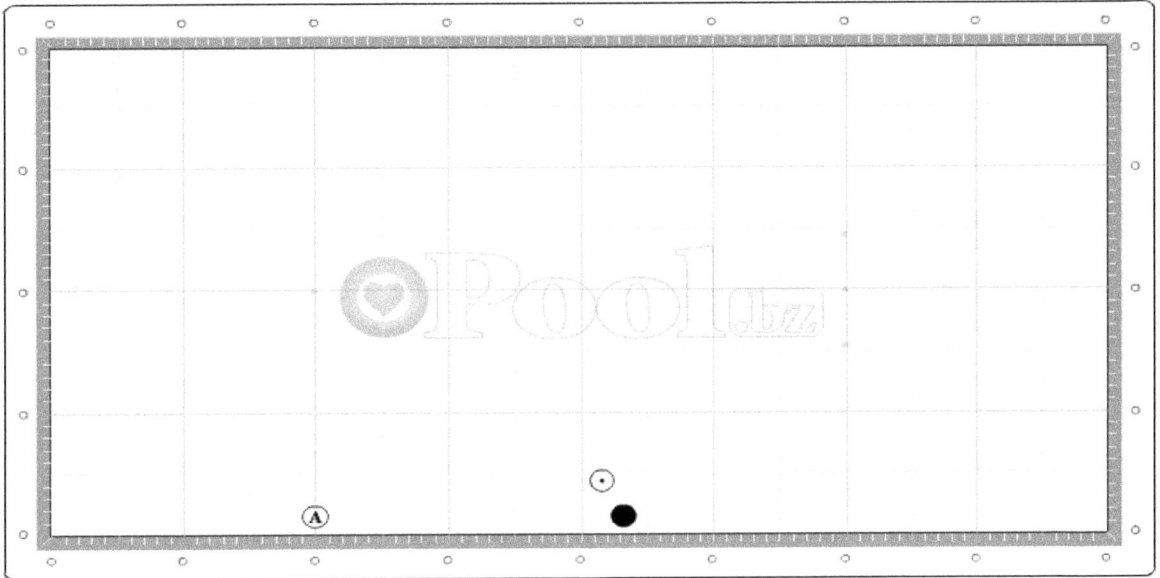

Shot Pattern

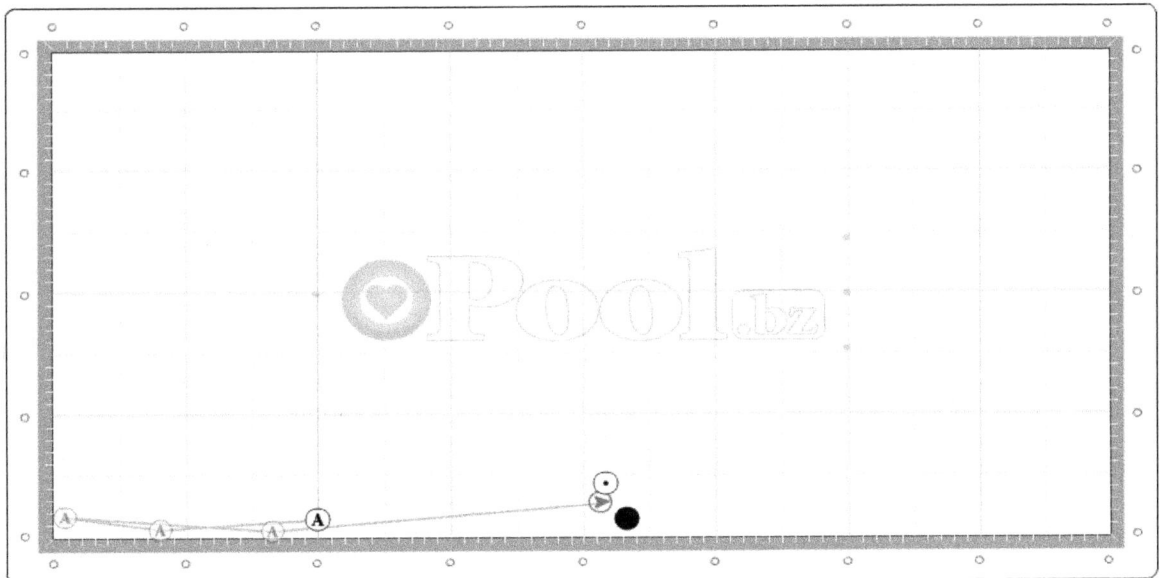

A:2b – Setup

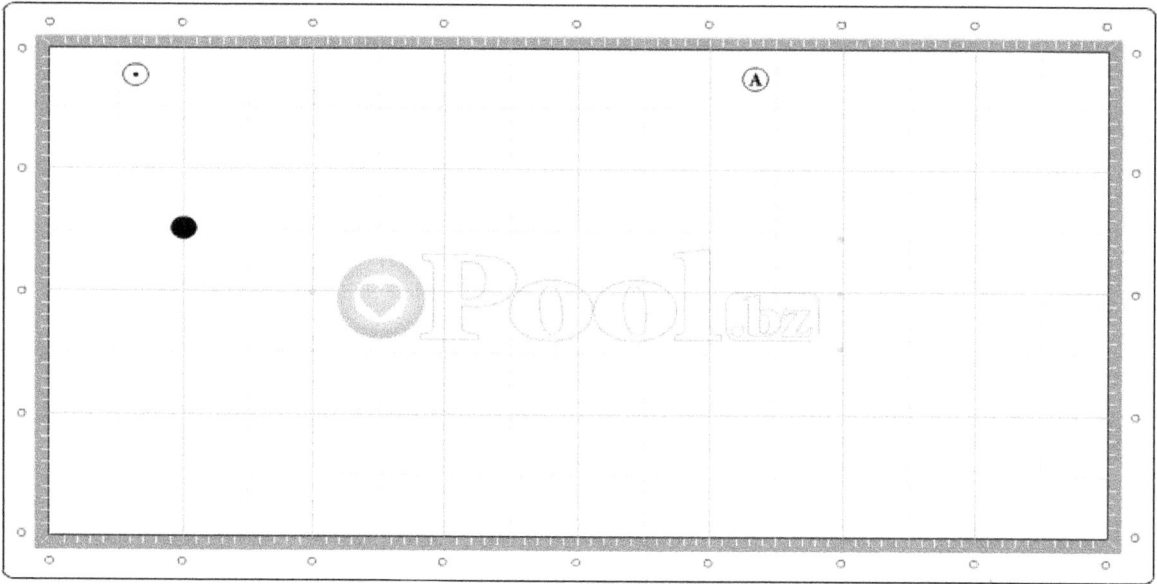

Shot Pattern

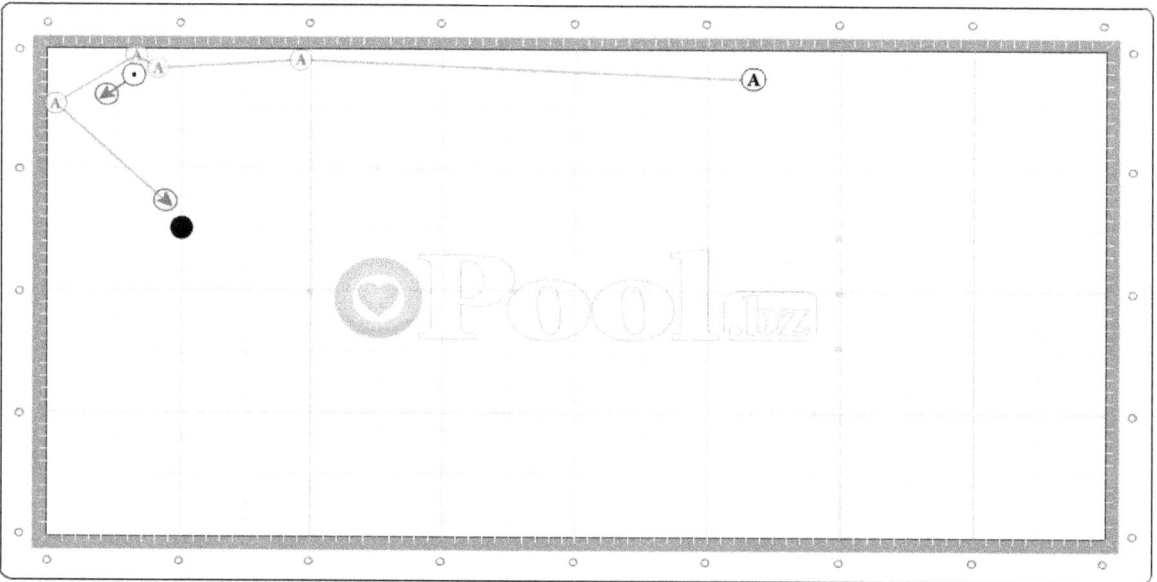

A:2c – Setup

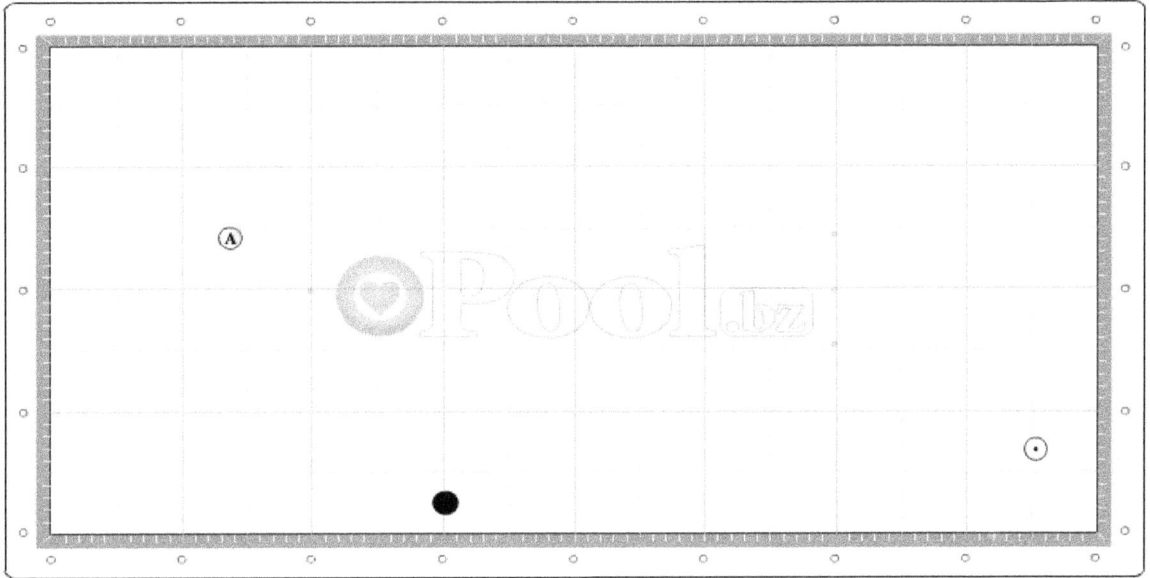

Shot Pattern

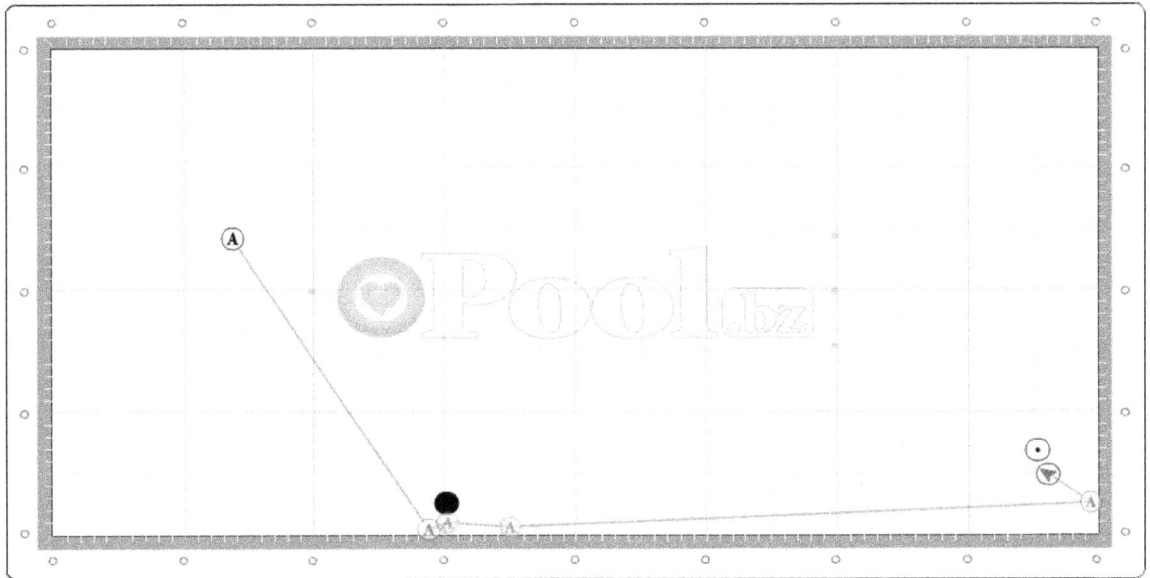

A:2d – Setup

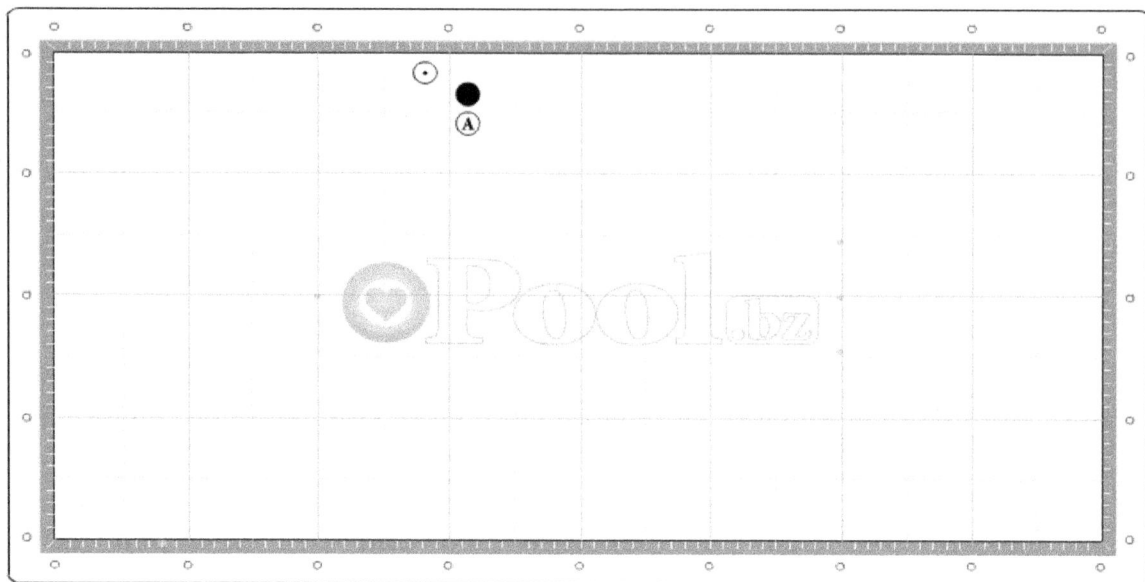

Shot Pattern

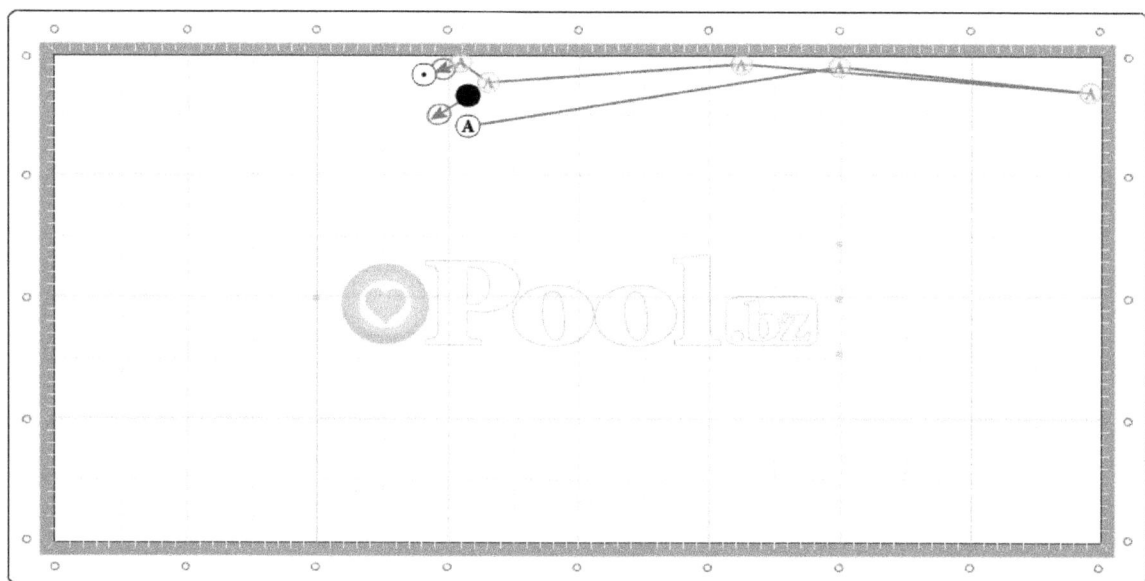

A: Group 3

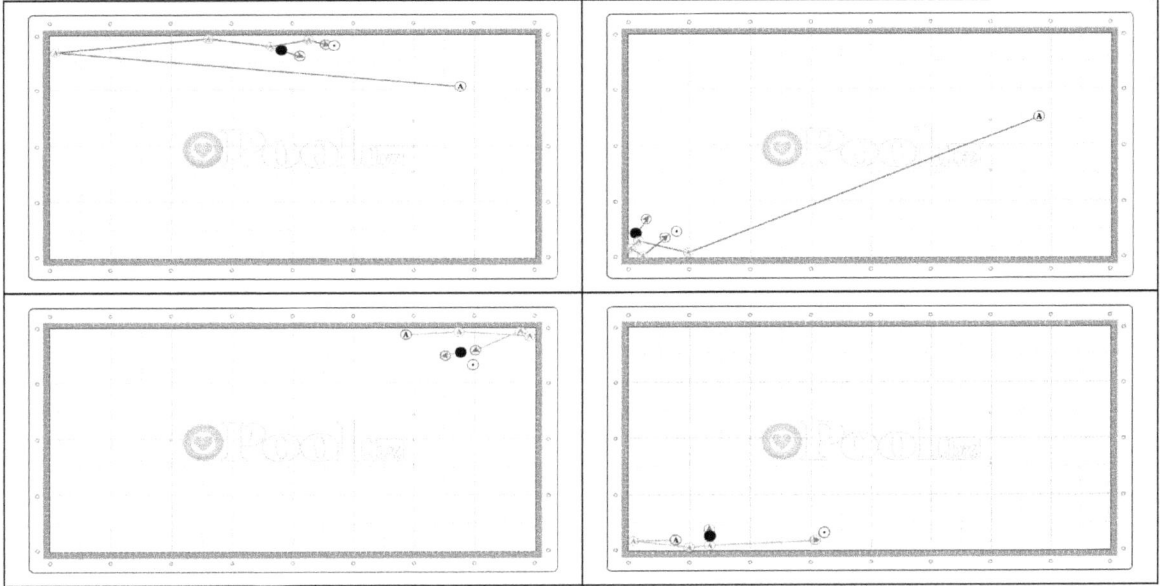

Analysis:

A:3a. _____

A:3b. _____

A:3c. _____

A:3d. _____

A:3a – Setup

Shot Pattern

A:3b – Setup

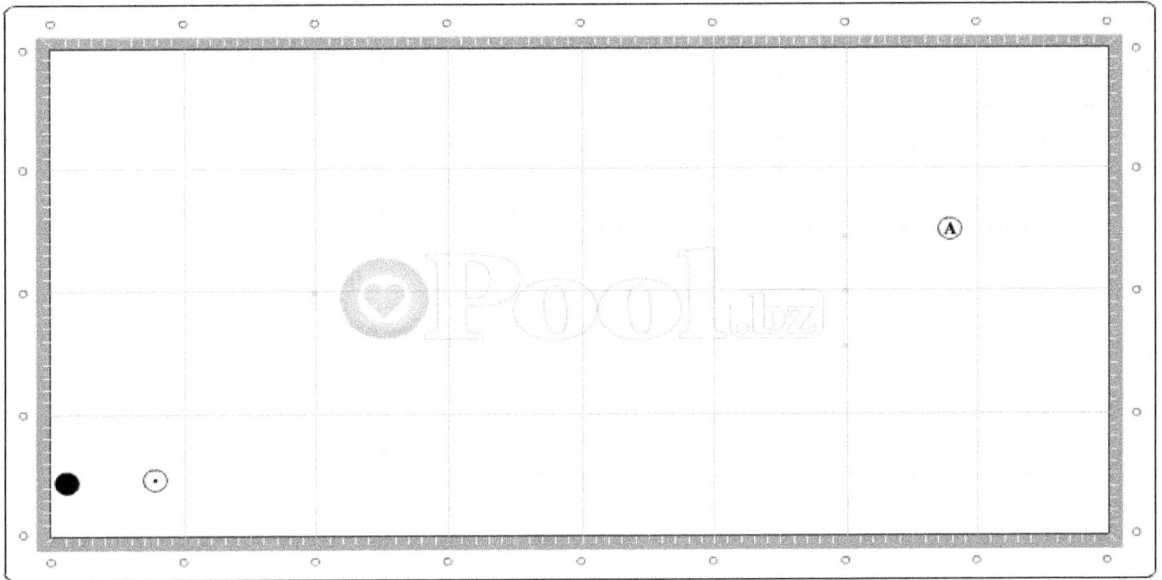

Shot Pattern

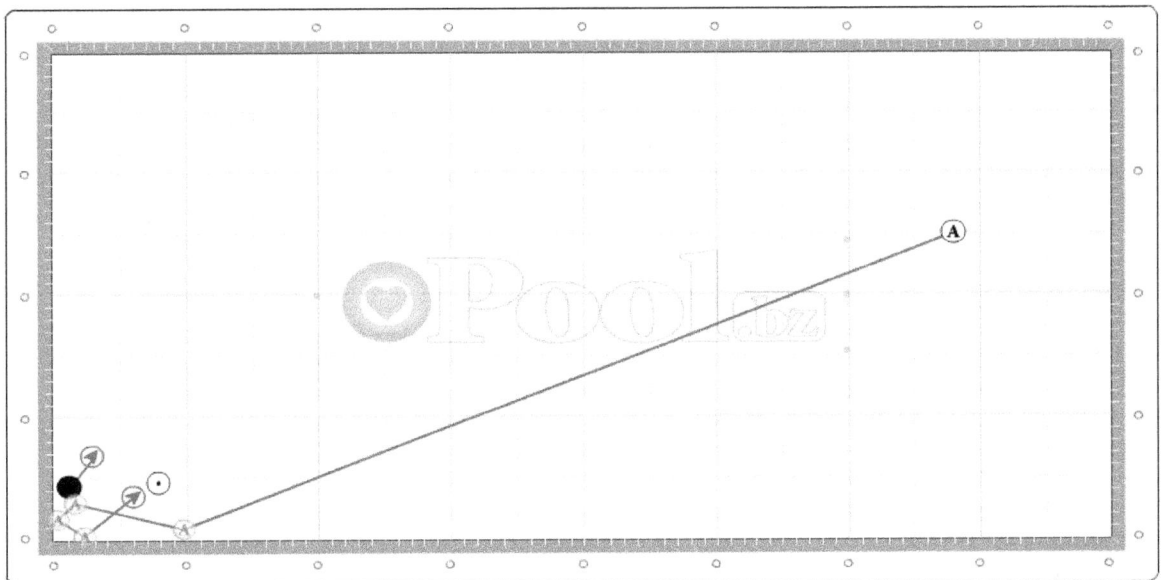

A:3c – Setup

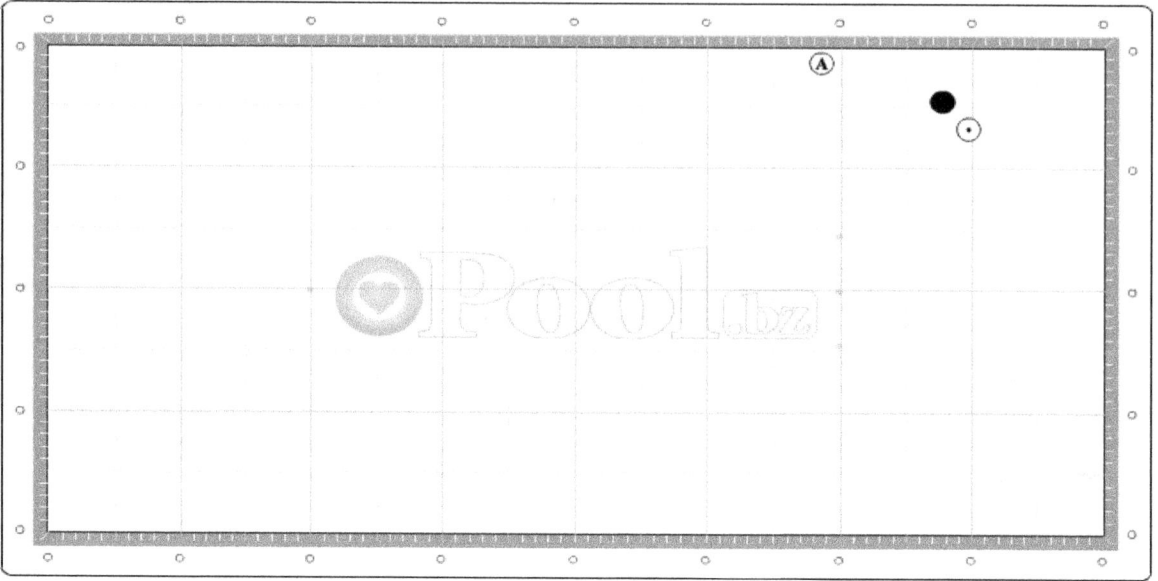

Shot Pattern

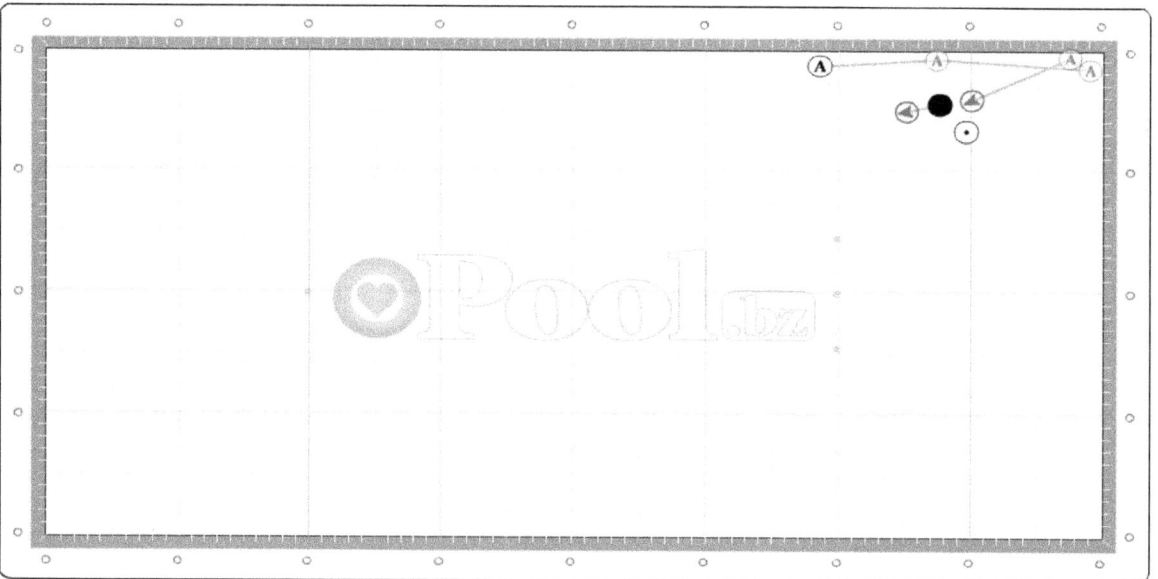

A:3d – Setup

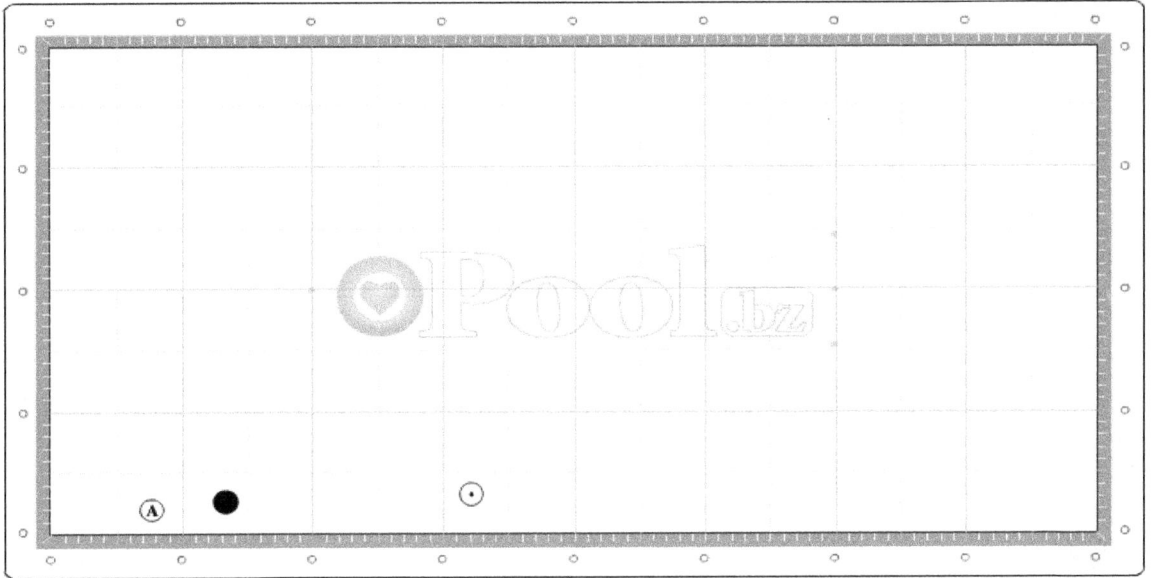

Shot Pattern

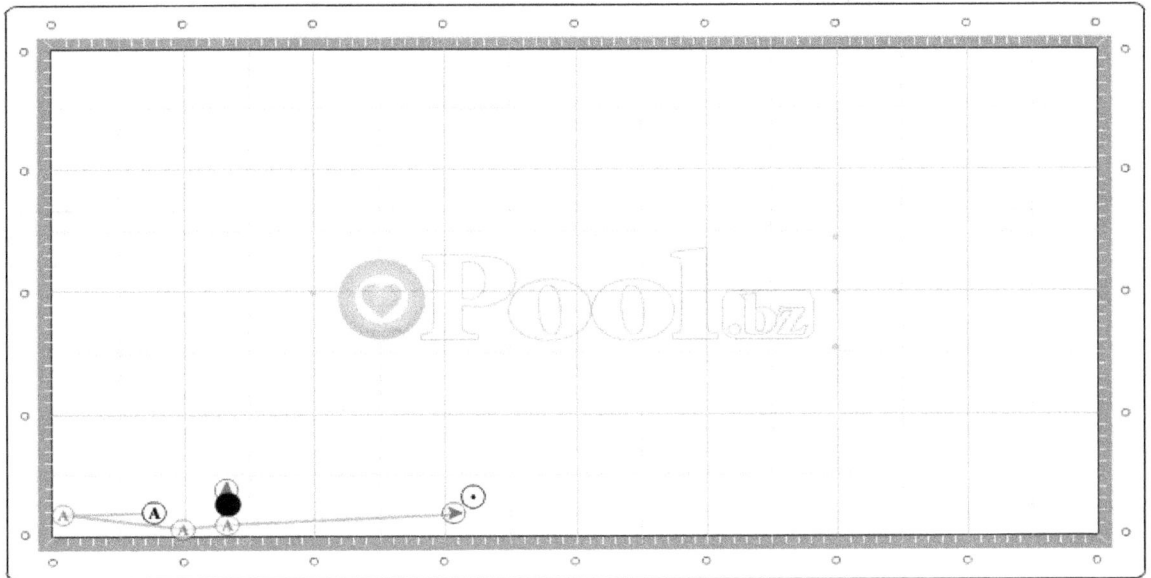

A: Group 4

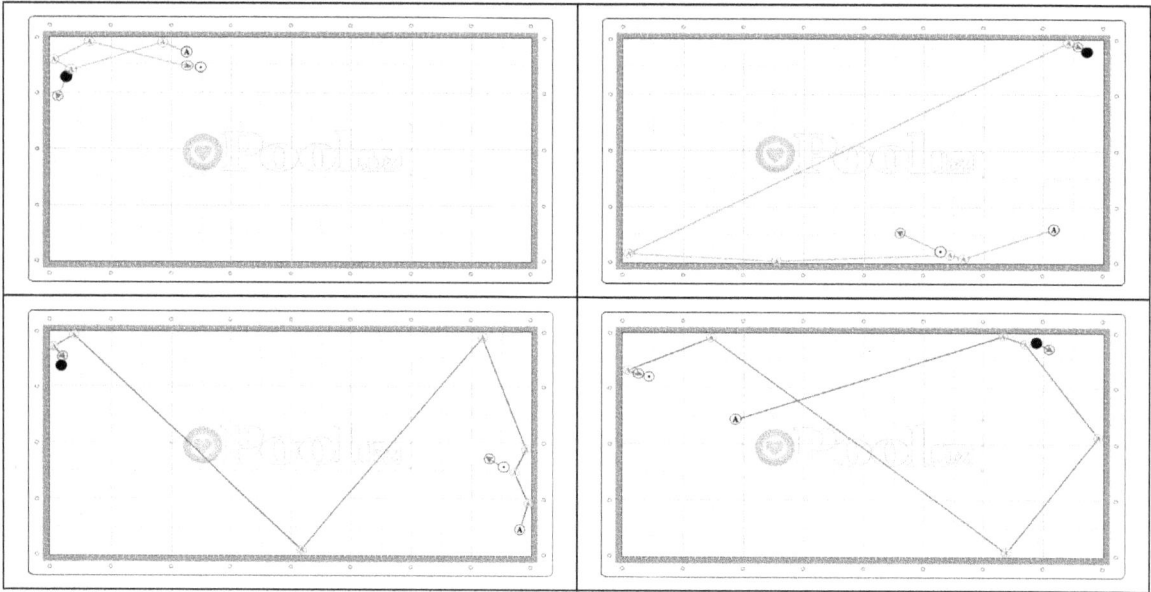

Analysis:

A:4a. _____

A:4b. _____

A:4c. _____

A:4d. _____

A:4a – Setup

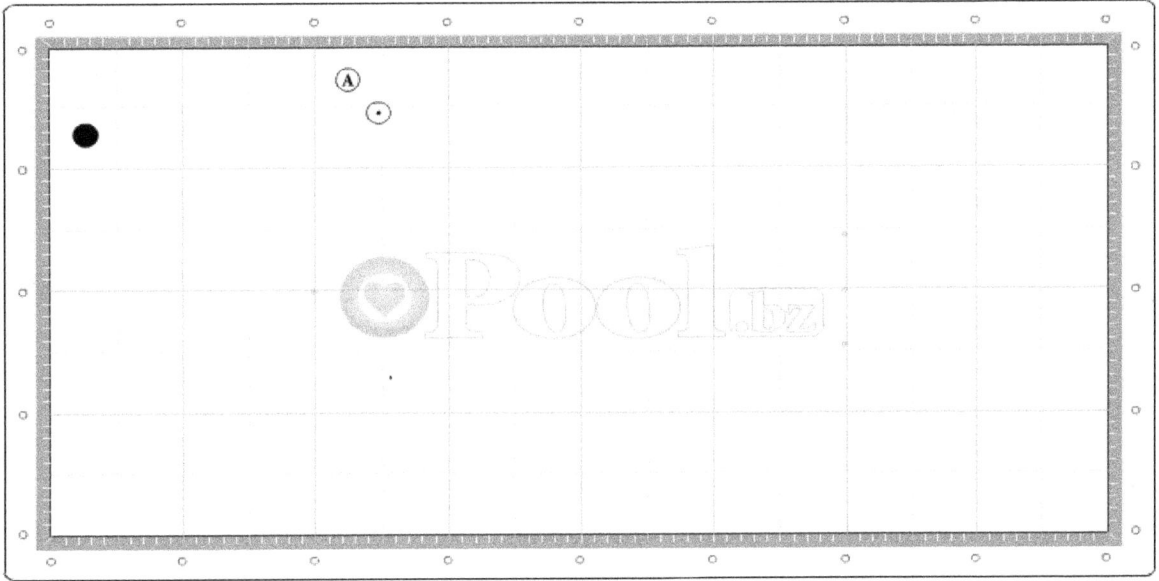

Shot Pattern

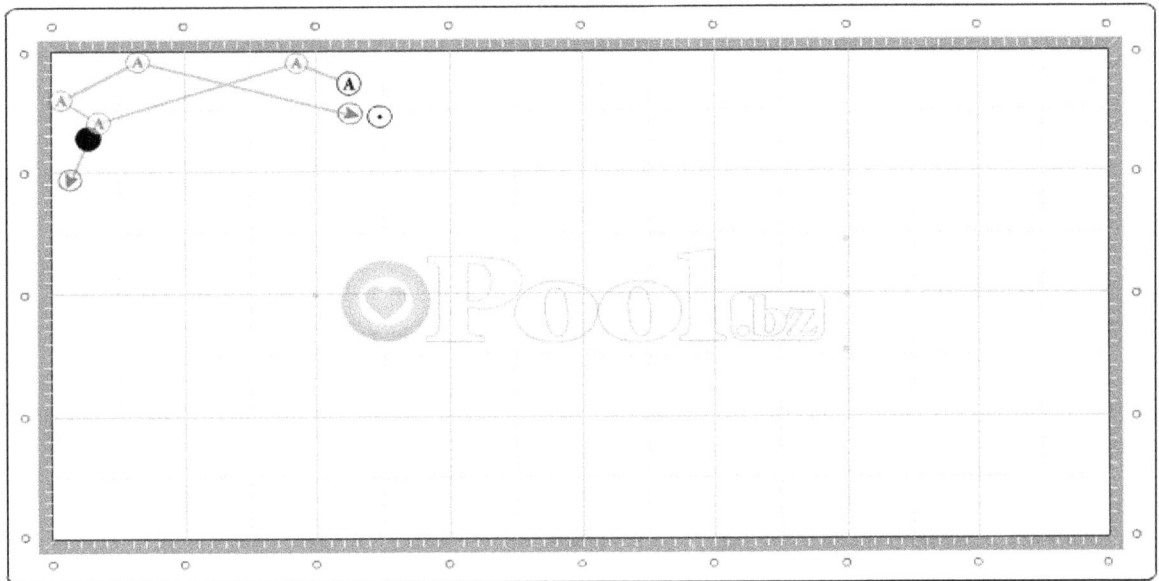

A:4b – Setup

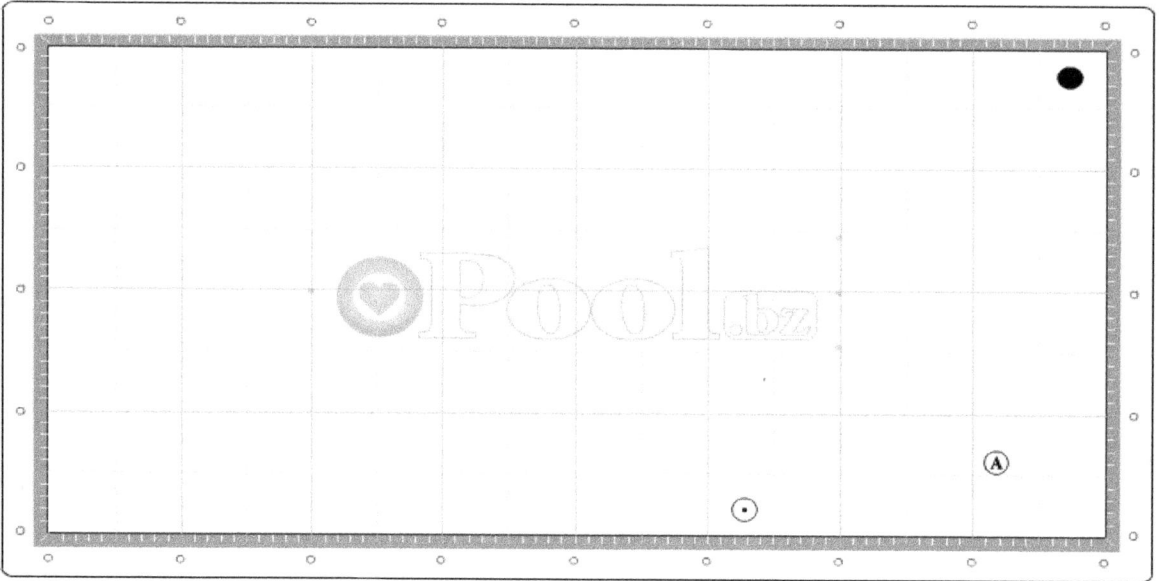

Shot Pattern

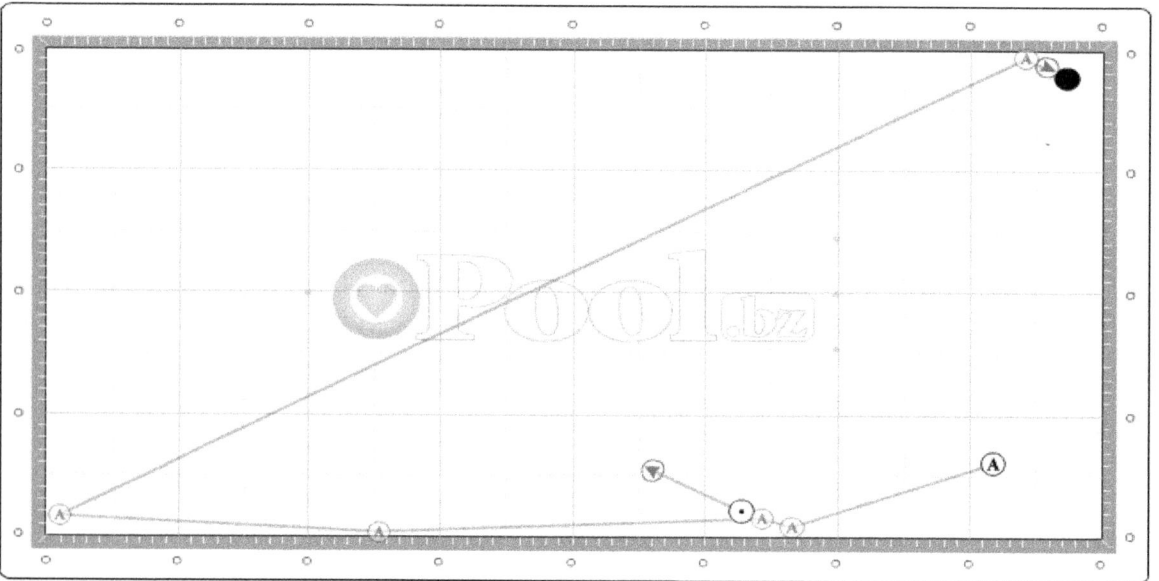

A:4c – Setup

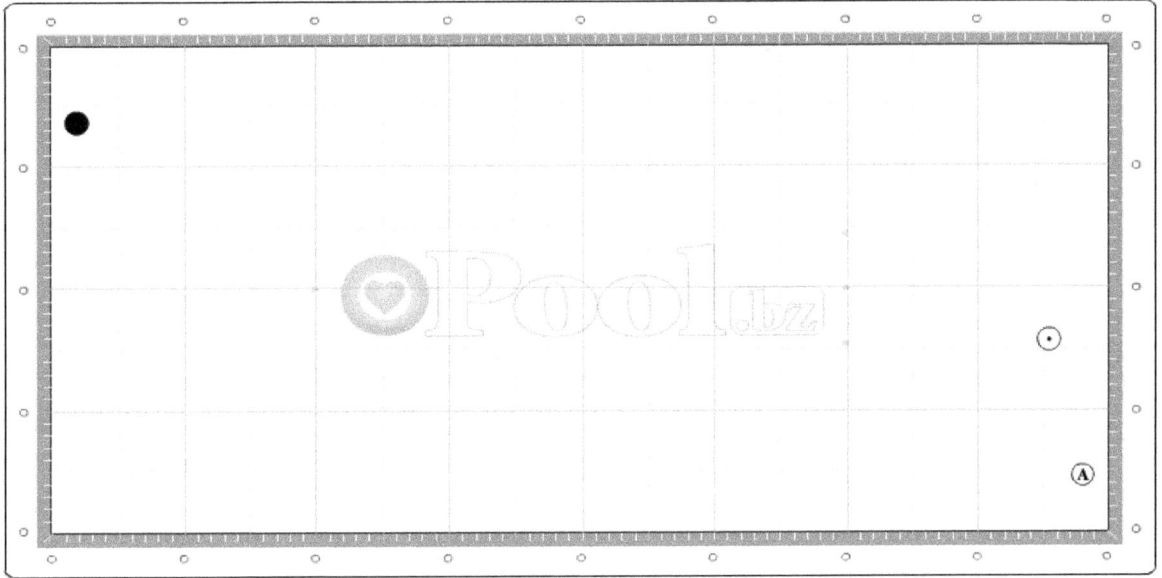

Shot Pattern

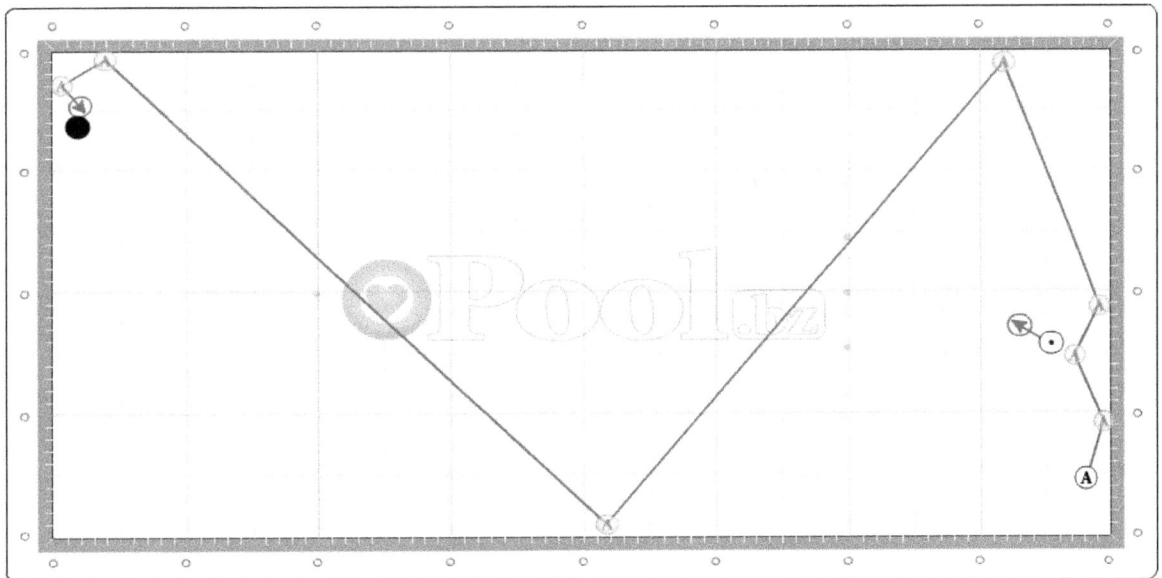

A:4d – Setup

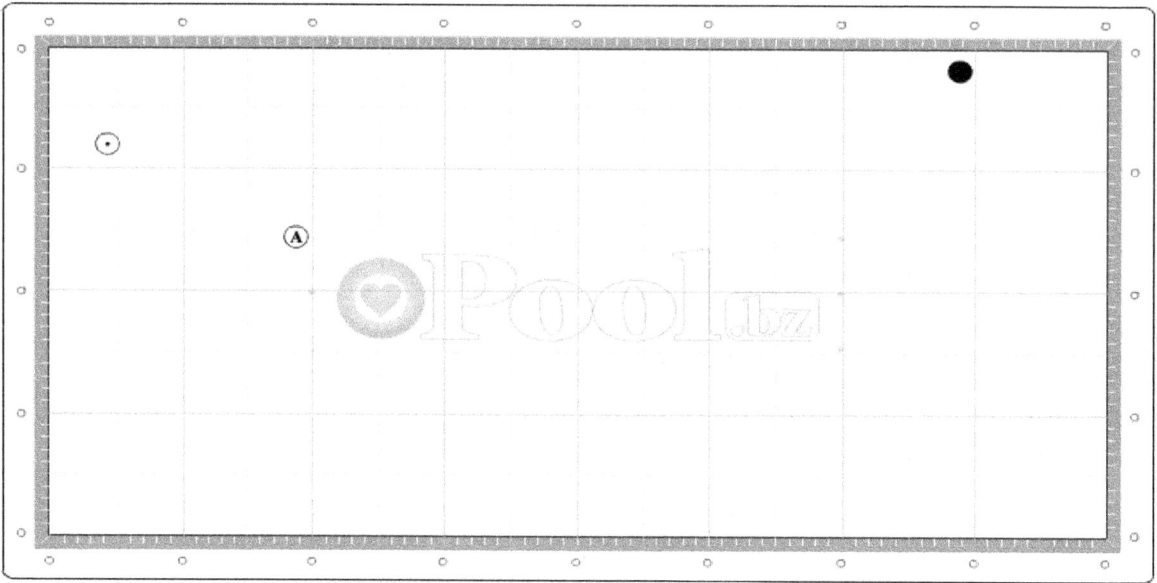

Shot Pattern

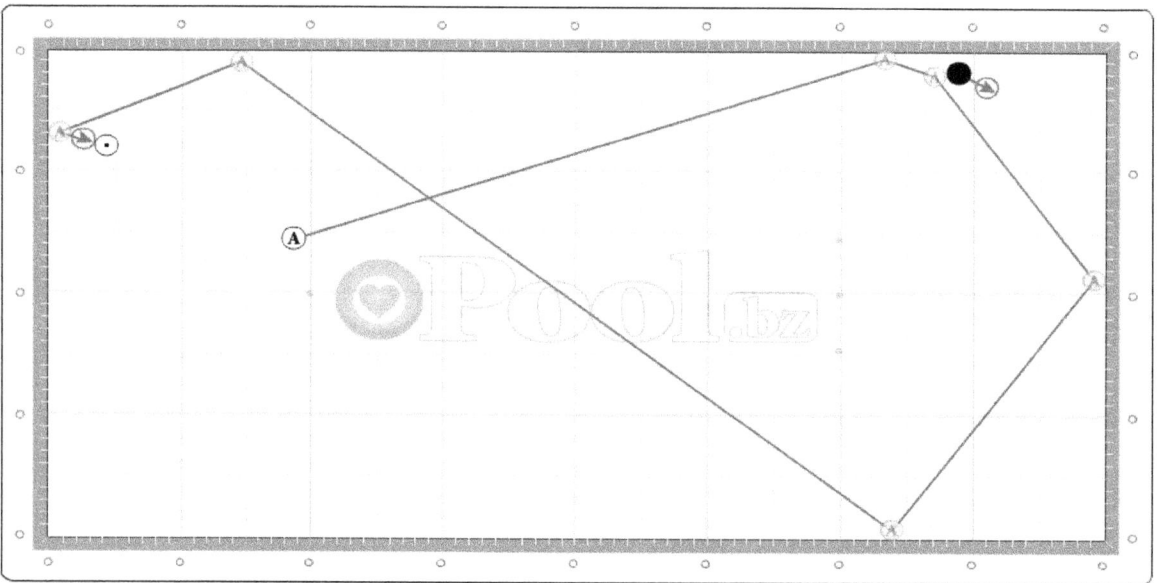

B: Up & Down the Rail

The CB makes a successful score while moving along one rail.

B: Group 1

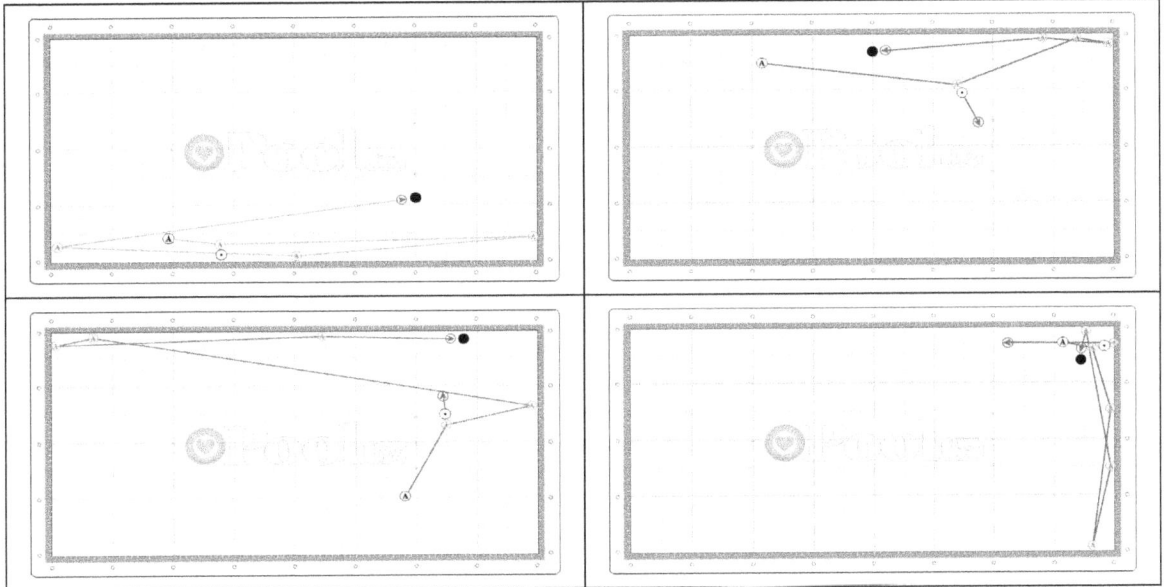

Analysis:

B:1a. _____

B:1b. _____

B:1c. _____

B:1d. _____

B:1a – Setup

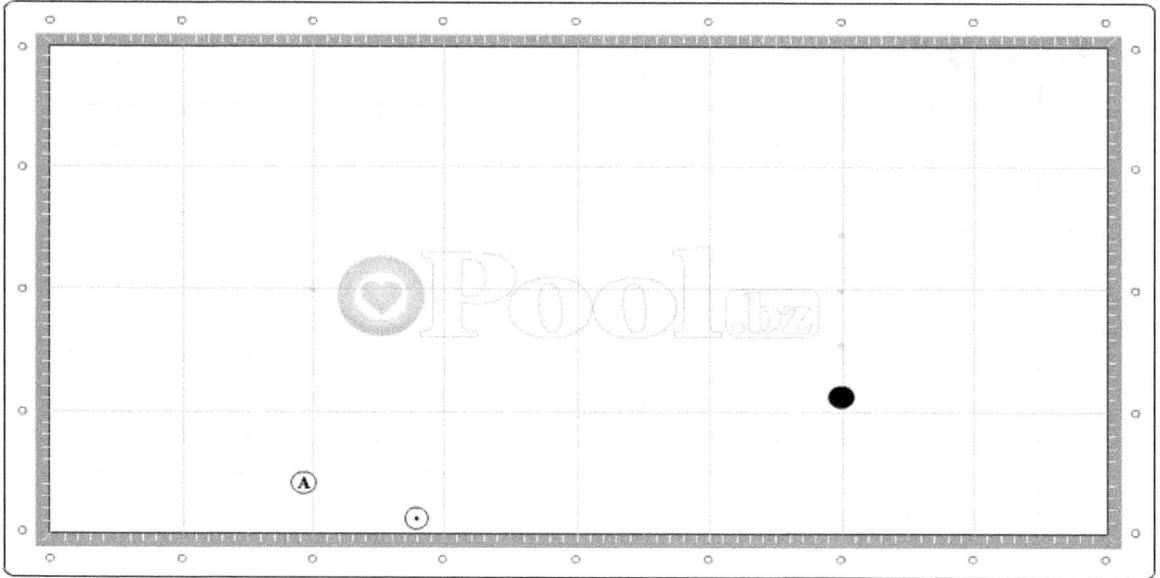

Shot Pattern

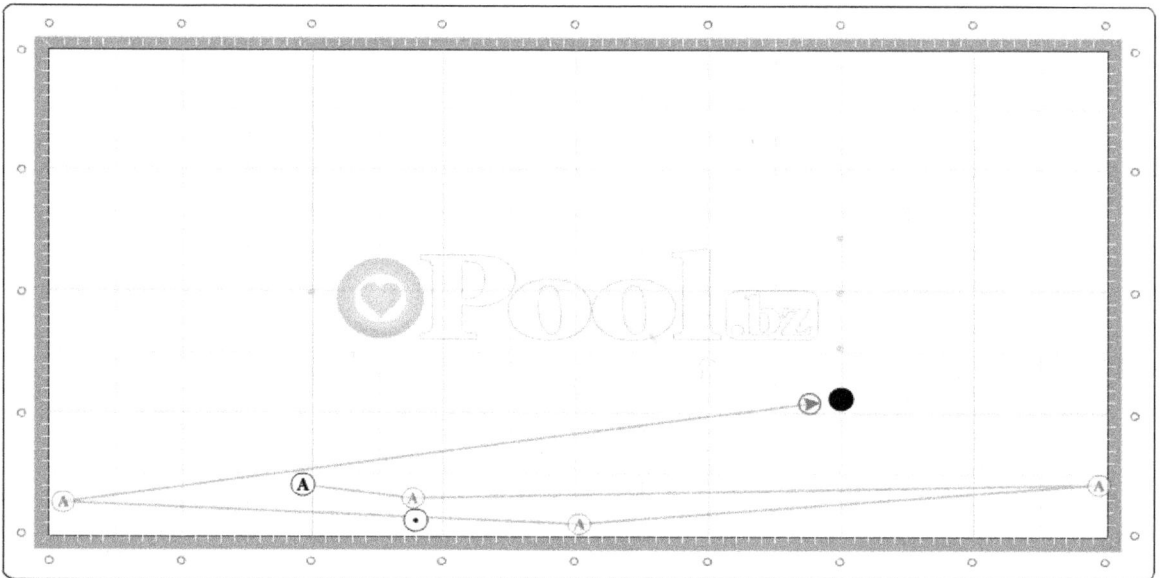

B:1b – Setup

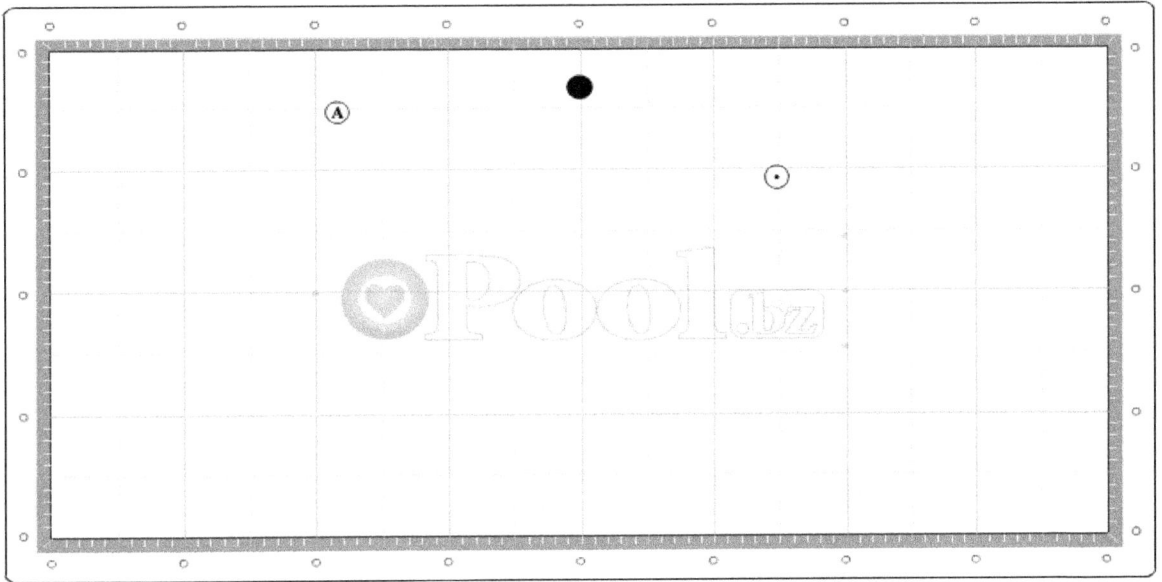

Shot Pattern

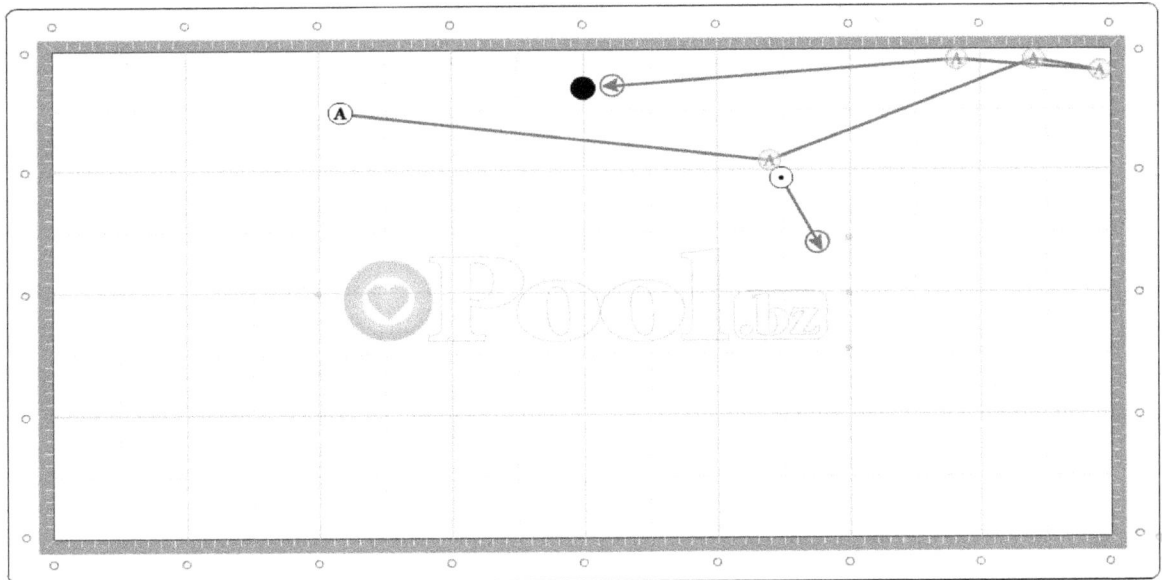

B:1c – Setup

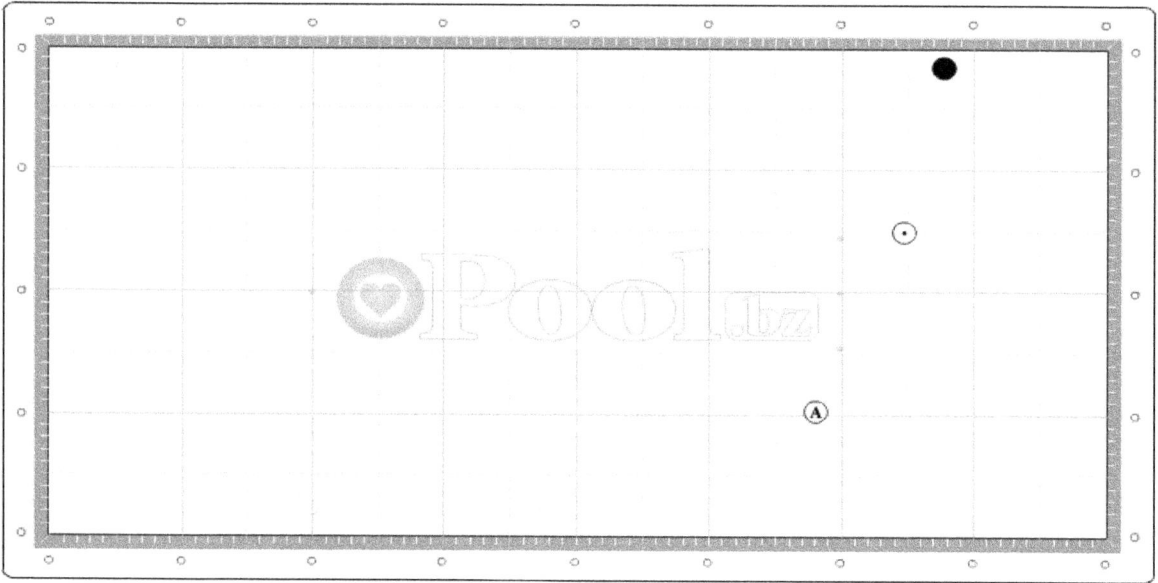

Shot Pattern

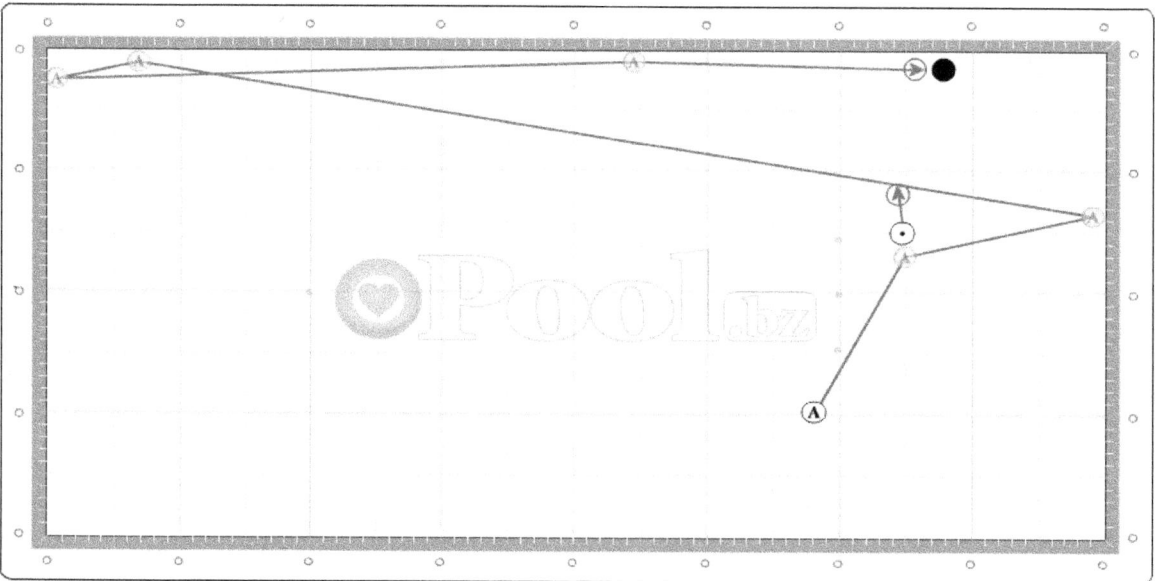

B:1d – Setup

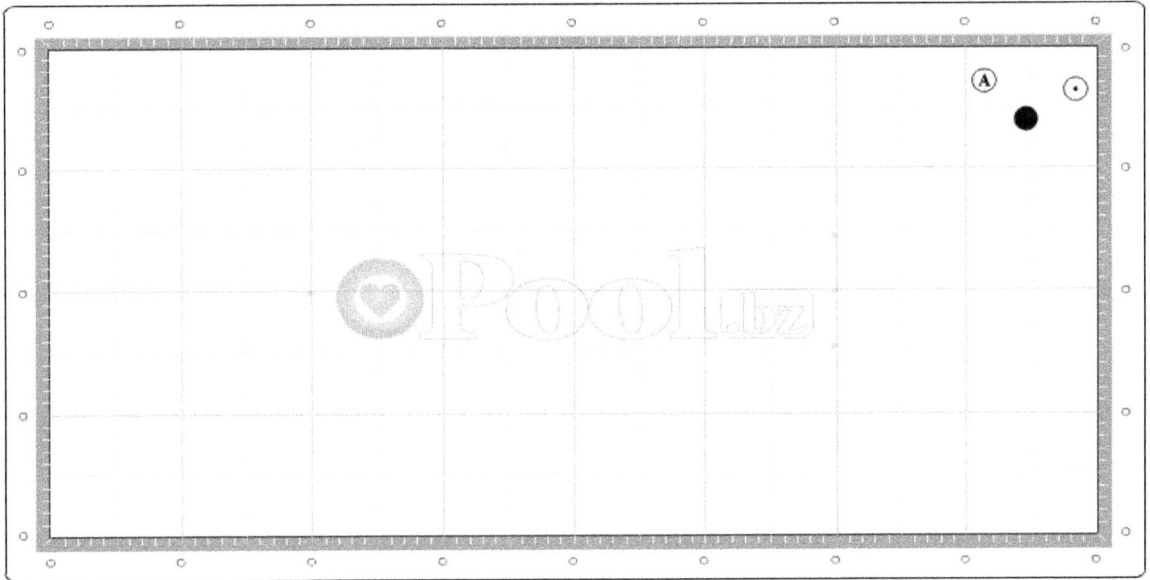

Shot Pattern

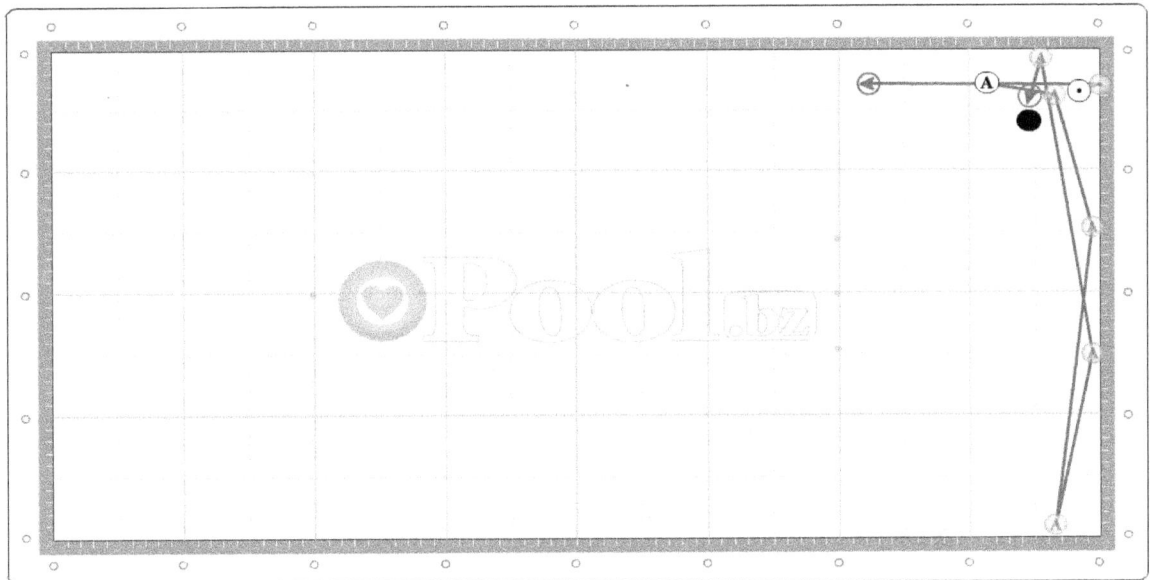

B: Group 2

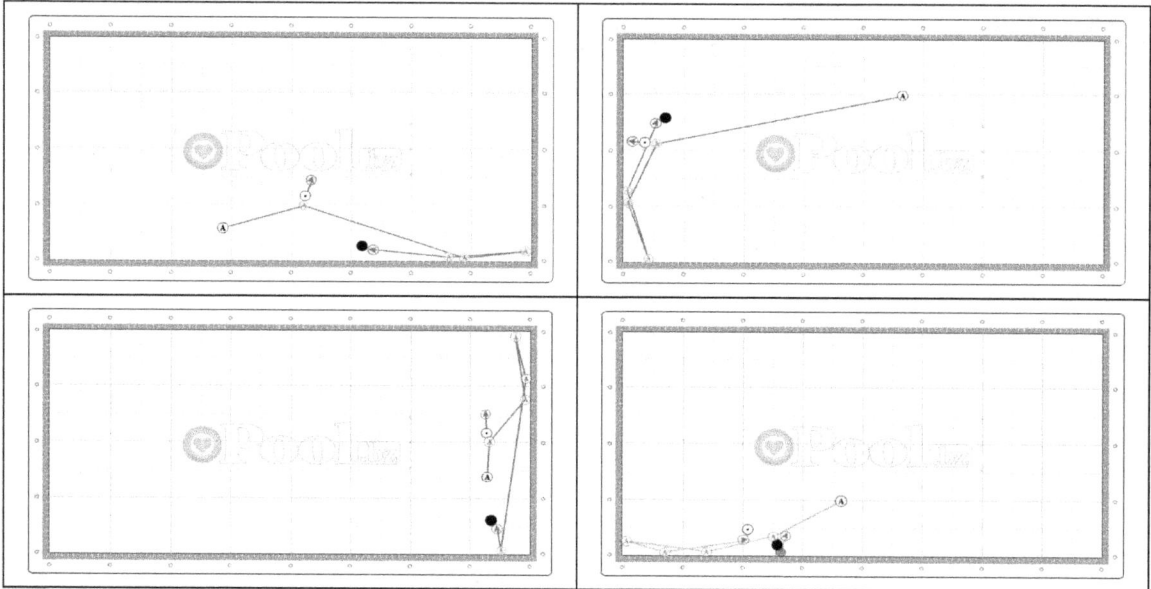

Analysis:

A:1a. _____

A:1b. _____

A:1c. _____

A:1d. _____

B:2a – Setup

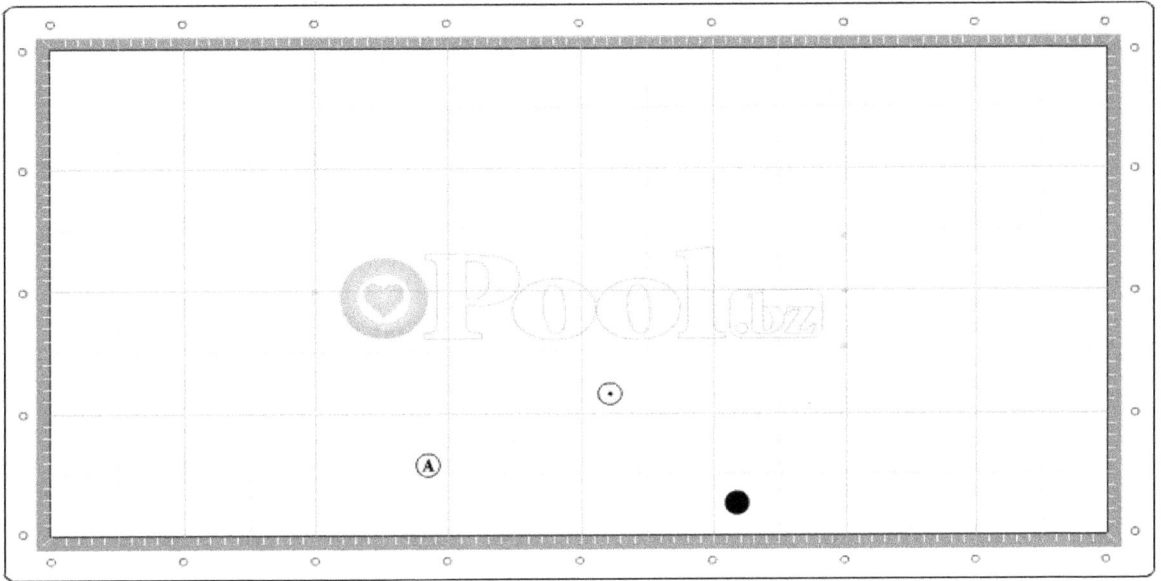

Shot Pattern

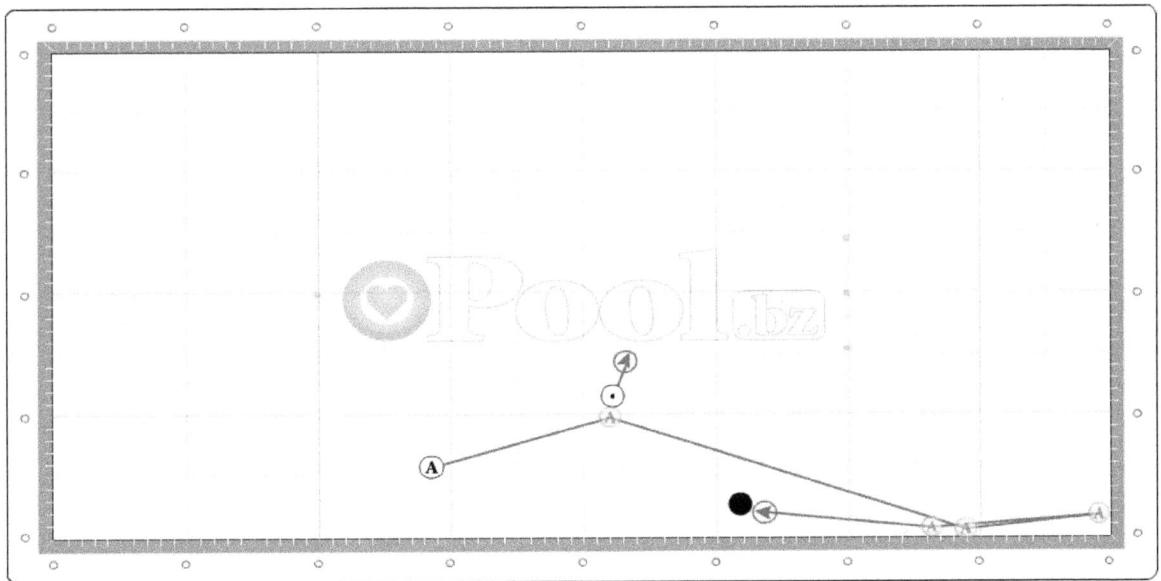

B:2b – Setup

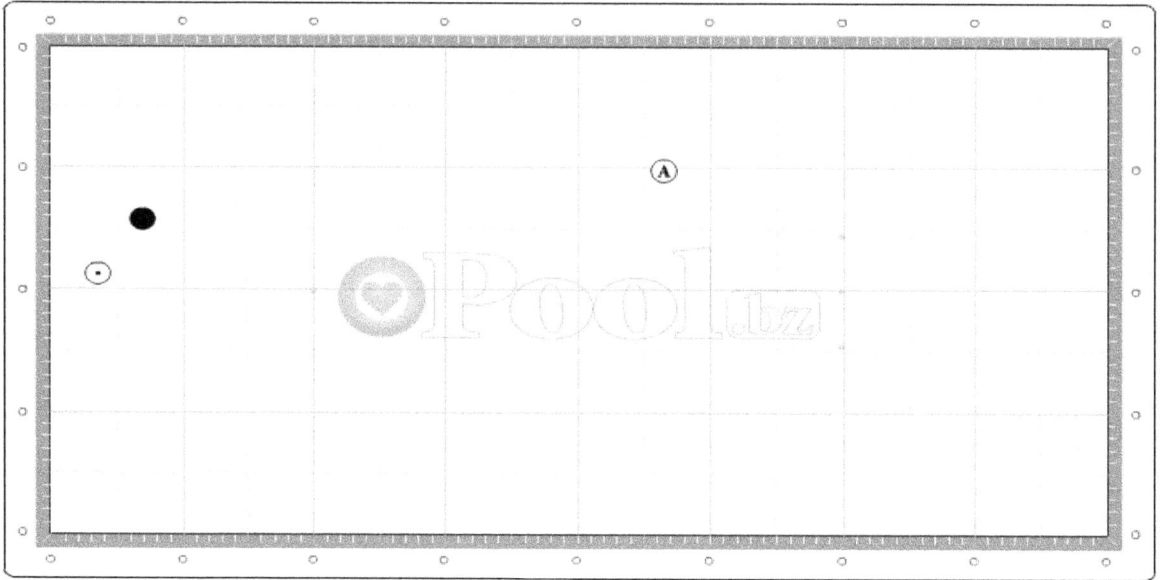

Shot Pattern

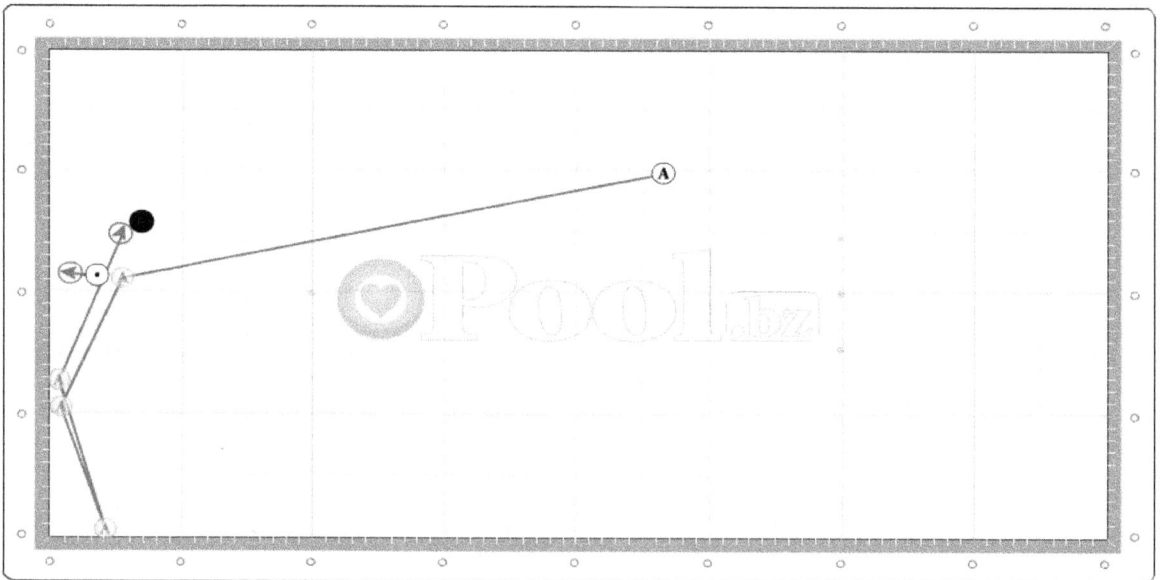

B:2c – Setup

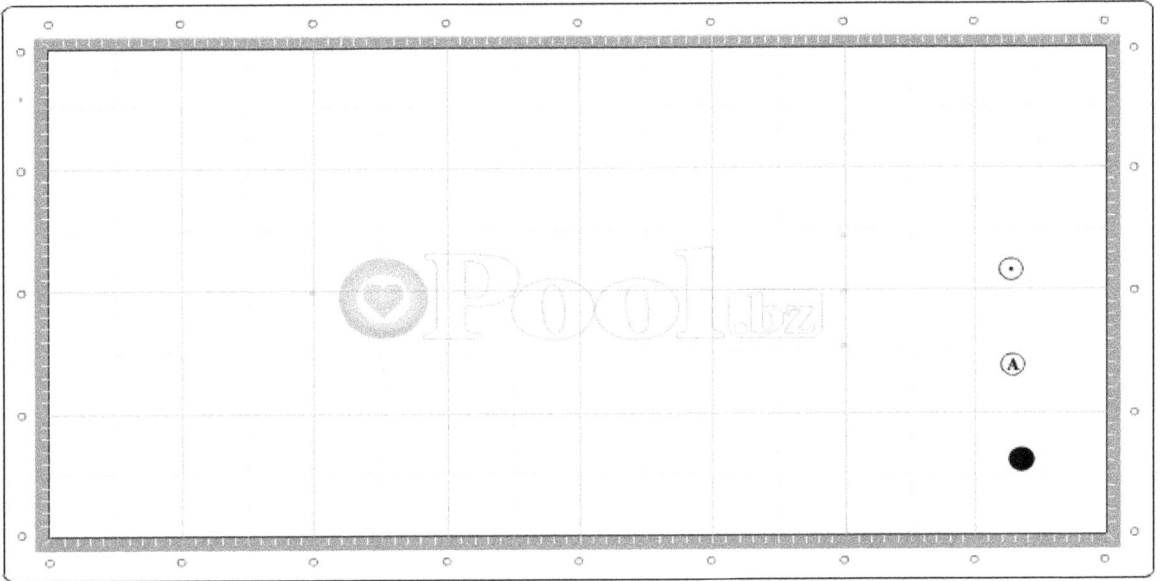

Shot Pattern

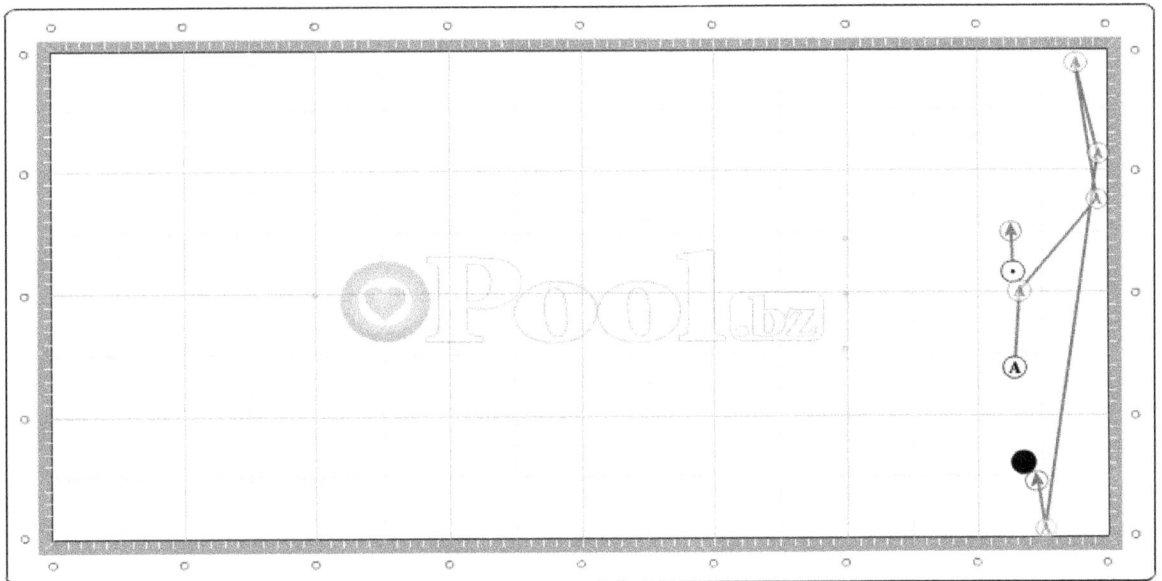

B:2d – Setup

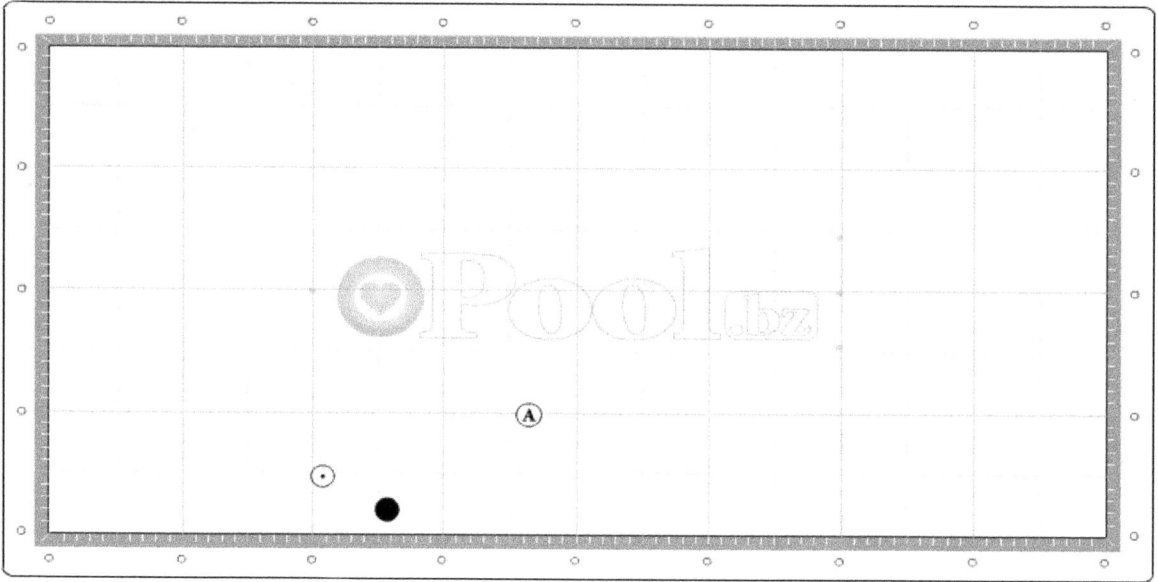

Shot Pattern

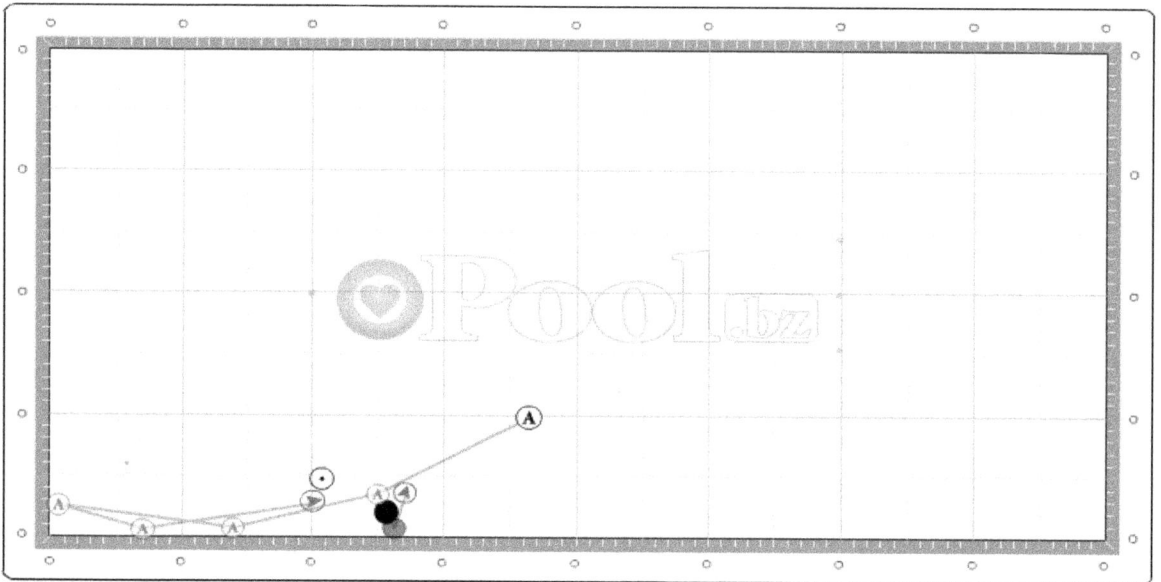

B: Group 3

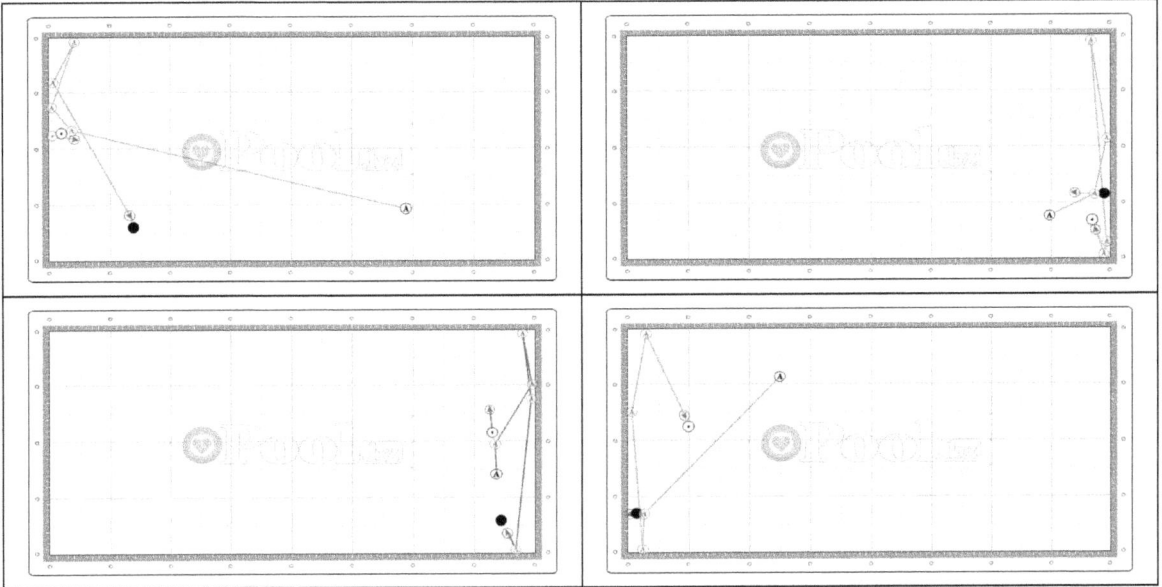

Analysis:

B:3a. _____

B:3b. _____

B:3c. _____

B:3d. _____

B:3a – Setup

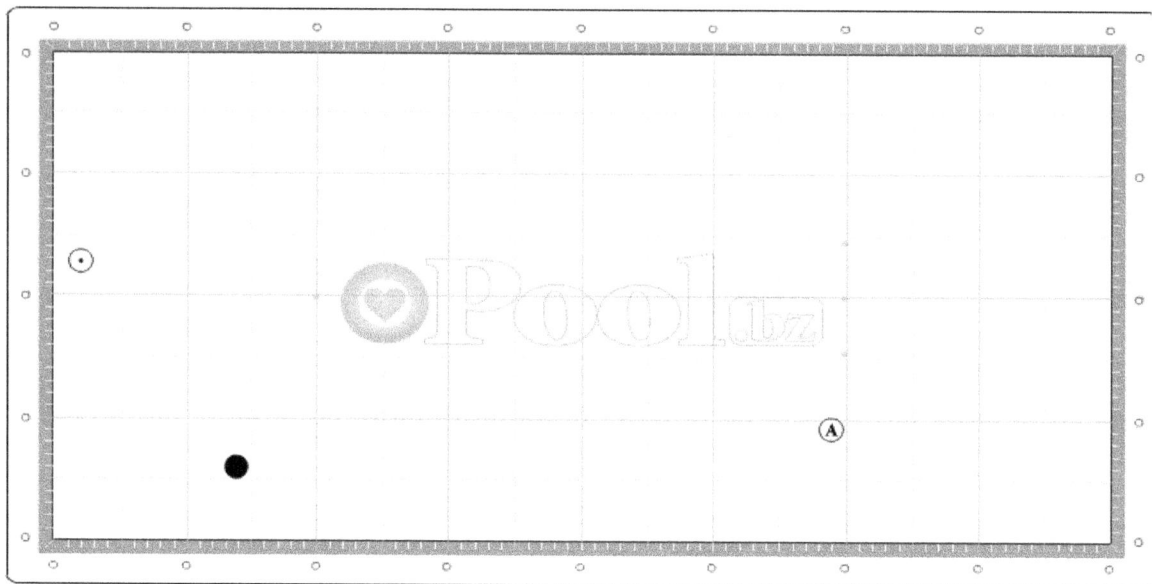

Shot Pattern

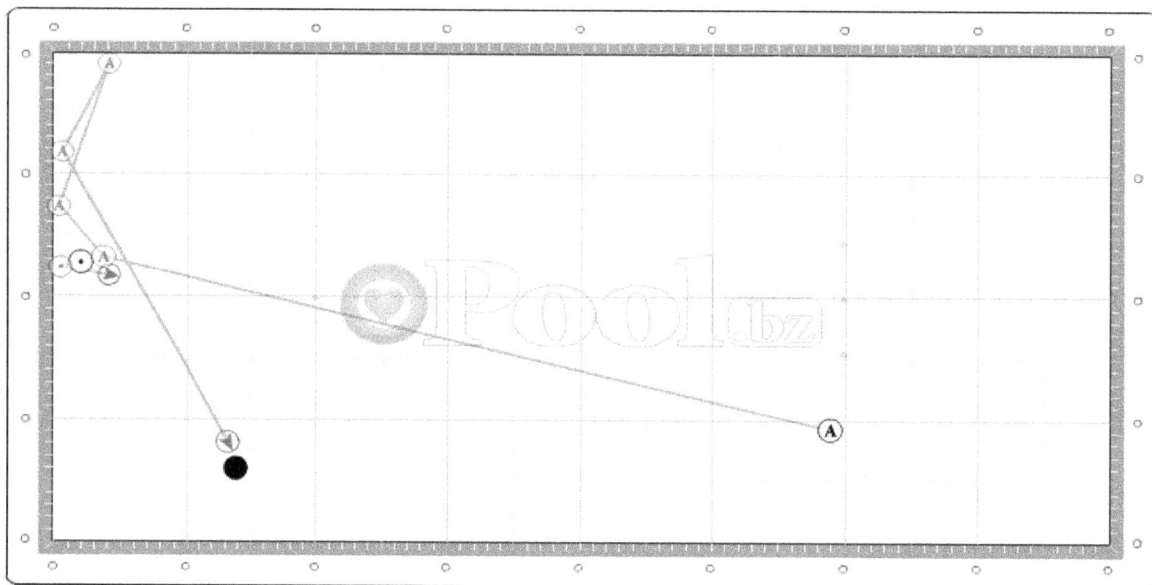

B:3b – Setup

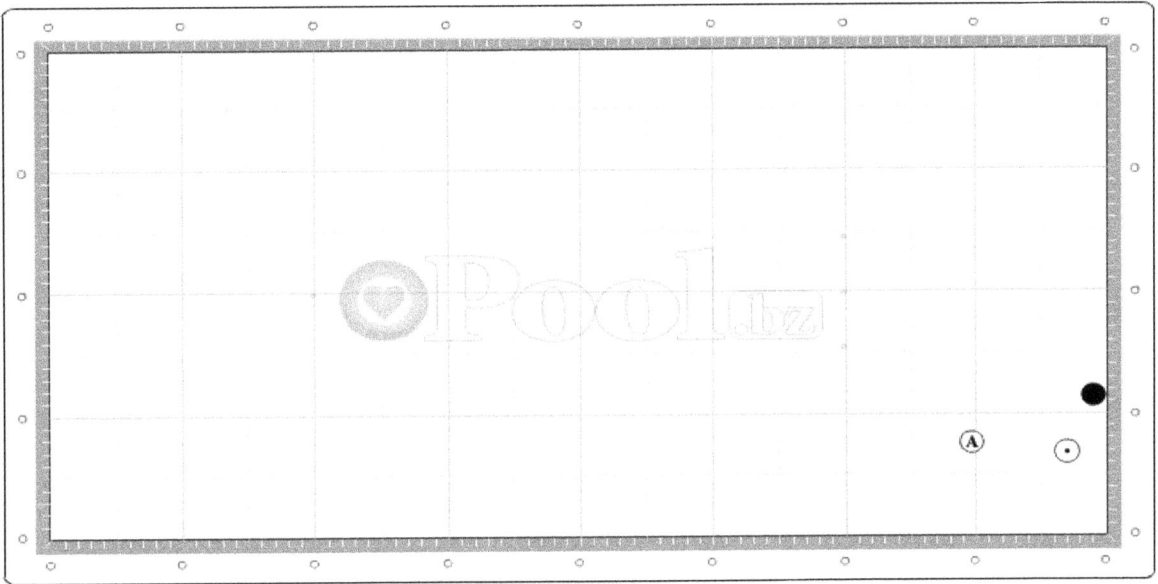

Shot Pattern

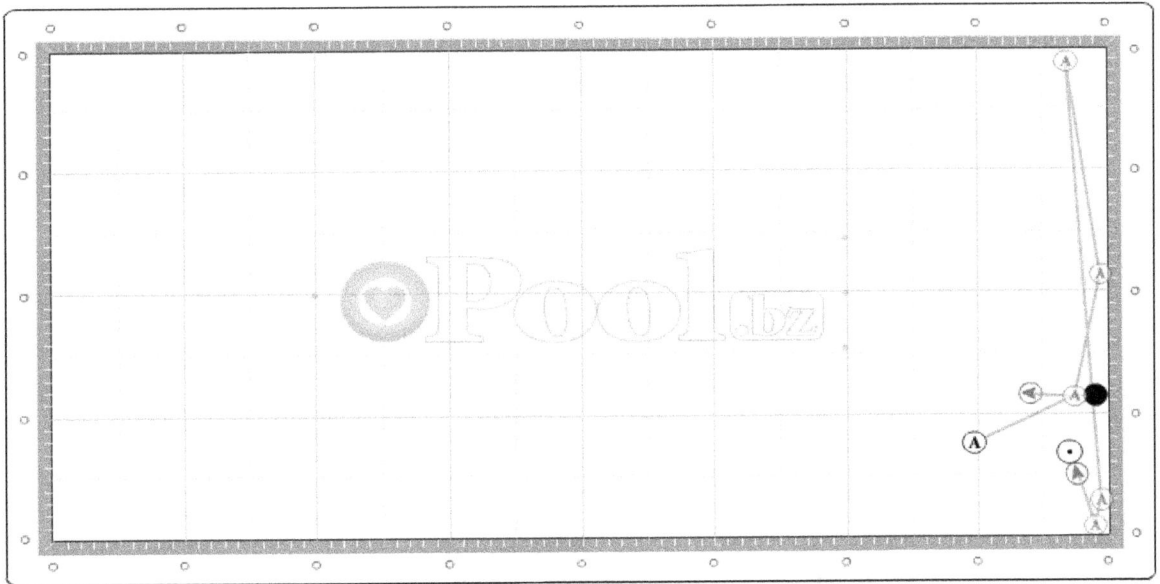

B:3c – Setup

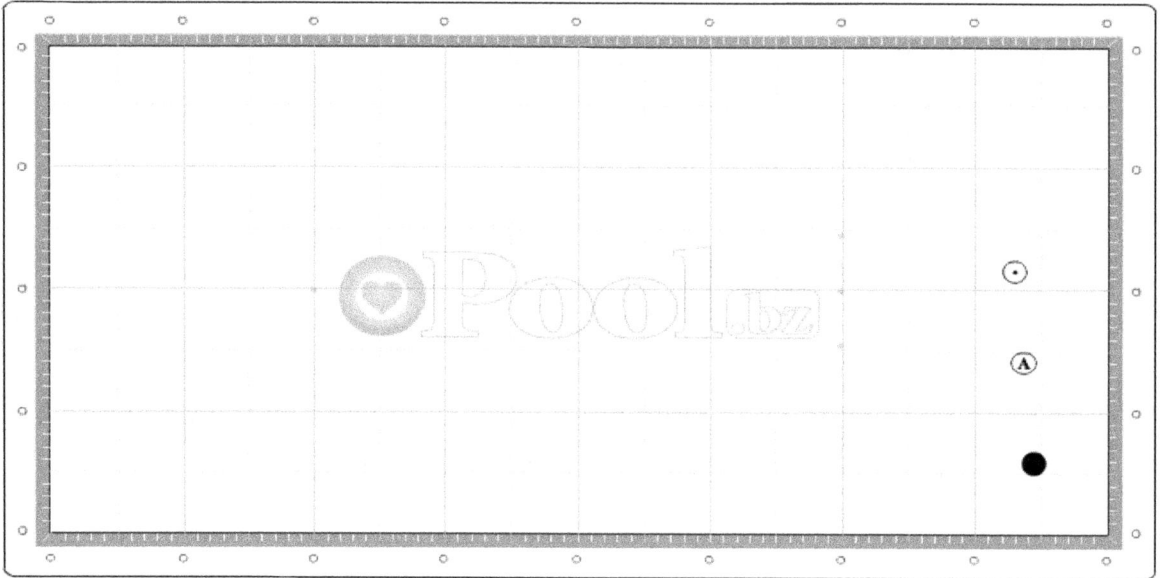

Shot Pattern

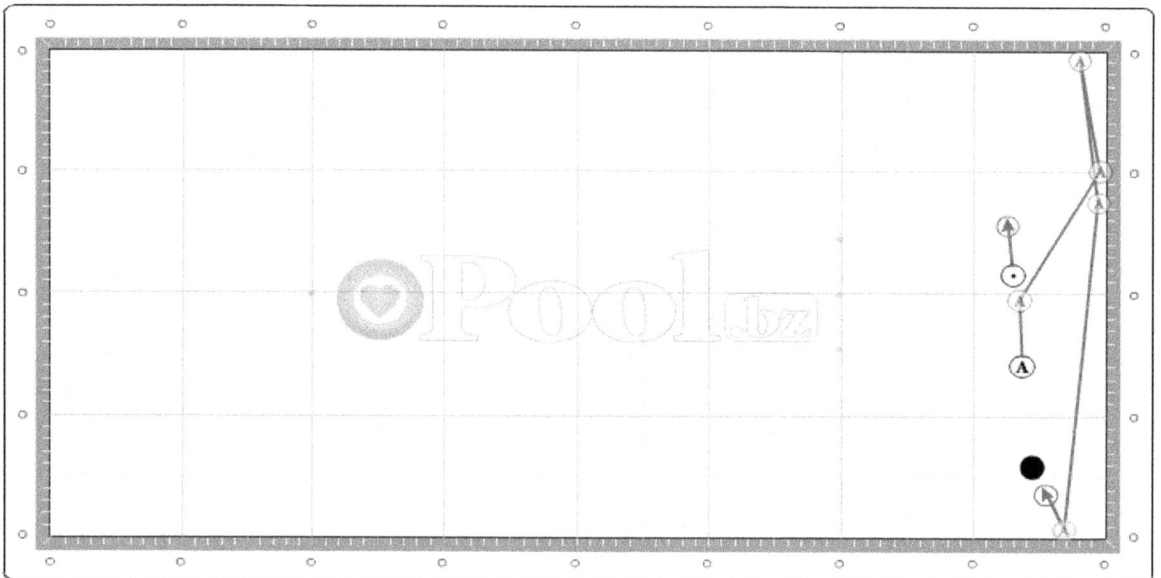

B:3d – Setup

Shot Pattern

B: Group 4

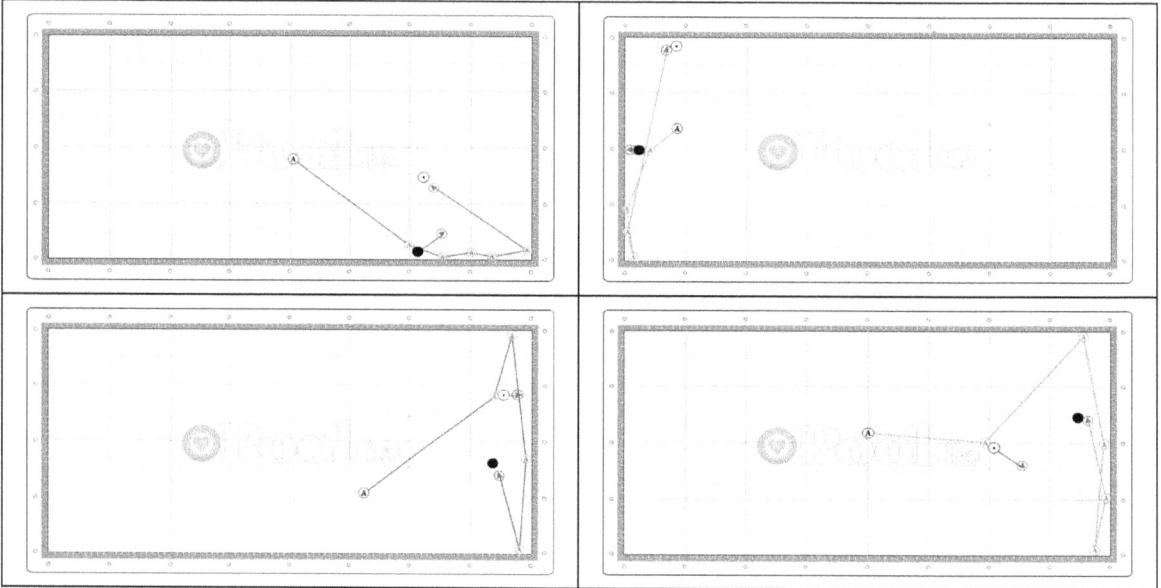

Analysis:

B:4a. _____

B:4b. _____

B:4c. _____

B:4d. _____

B:4a – Setup

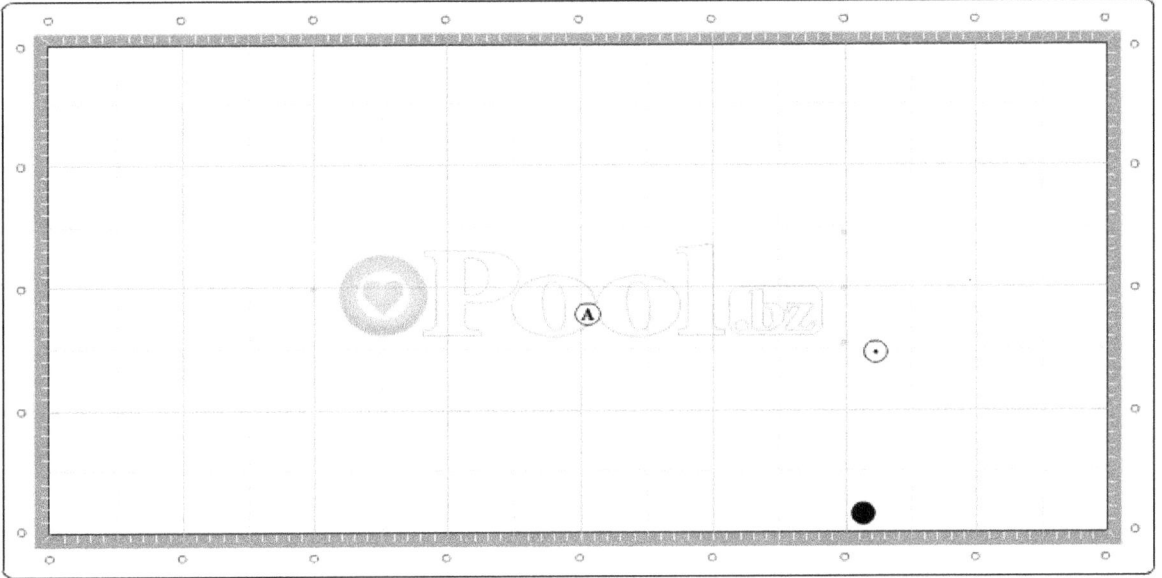

Shot Pattern

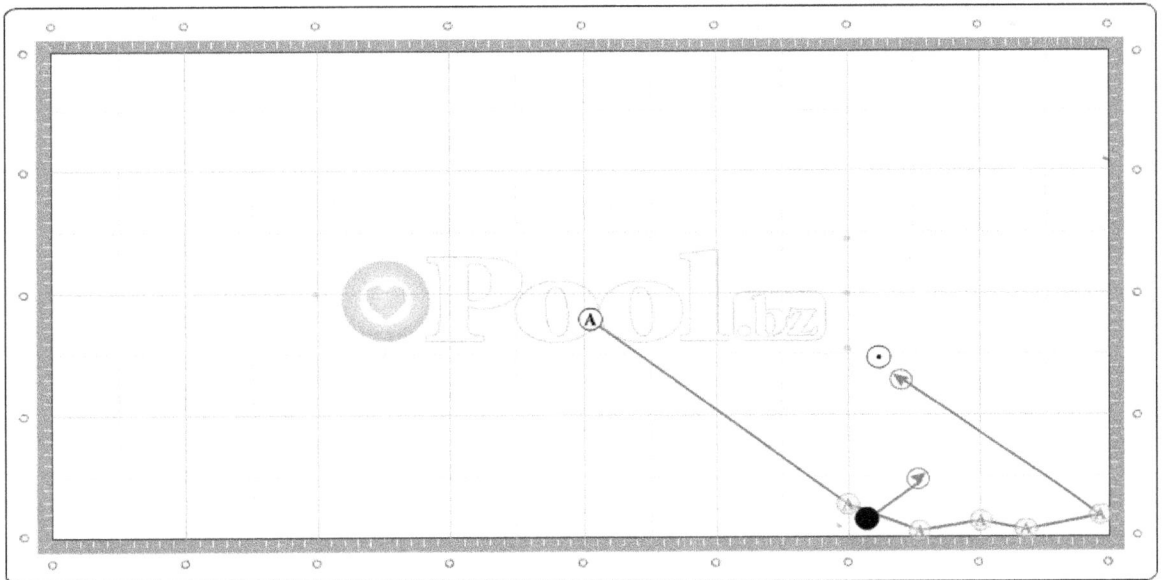

B:4b – Setup

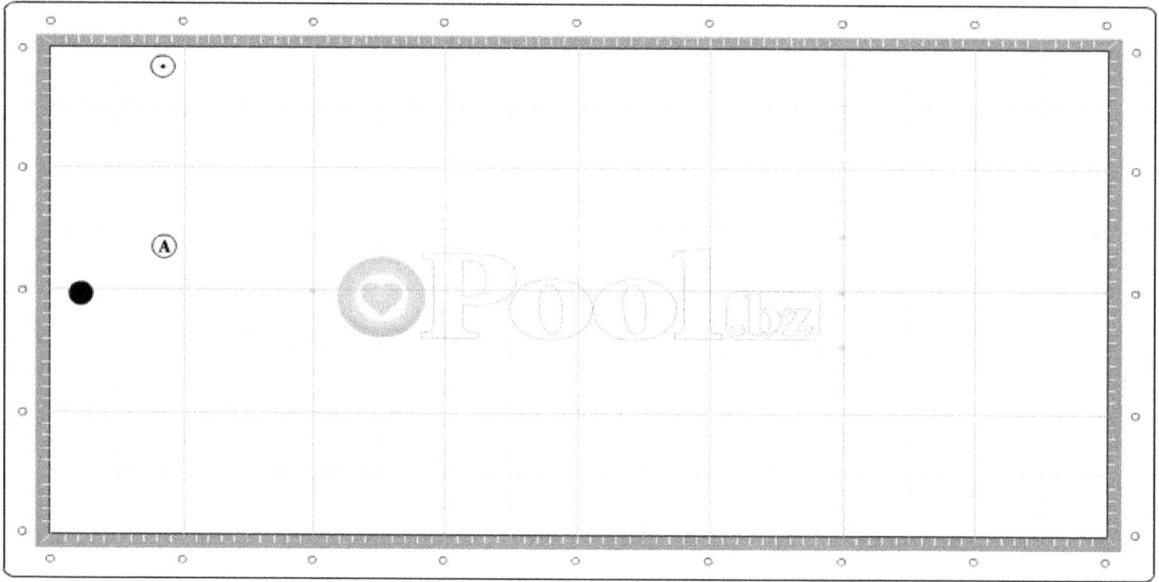

Shot Pattern

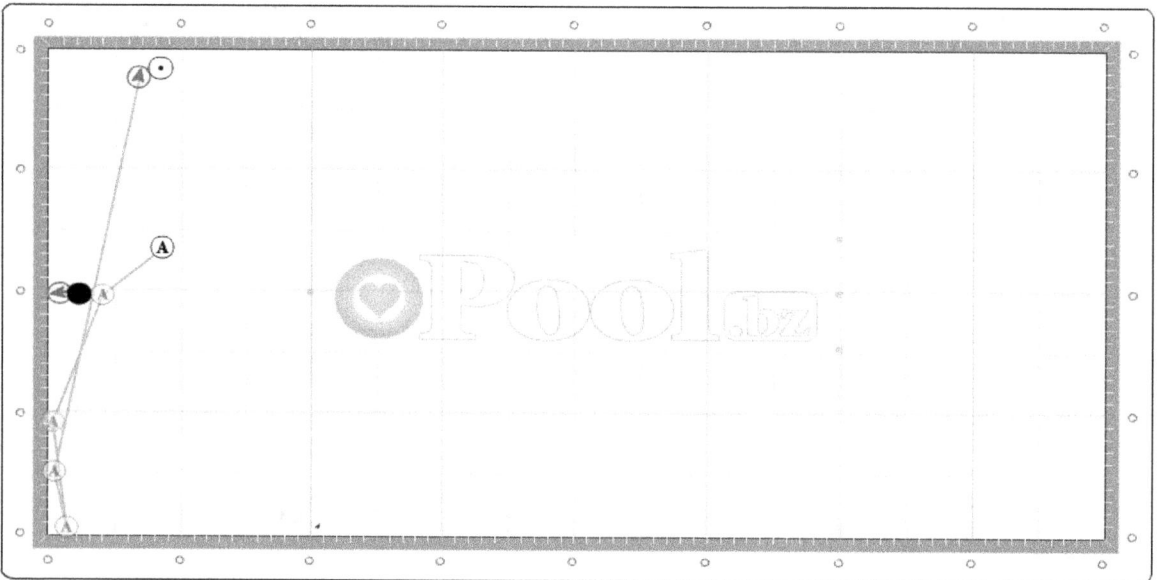

B:4c – Setup

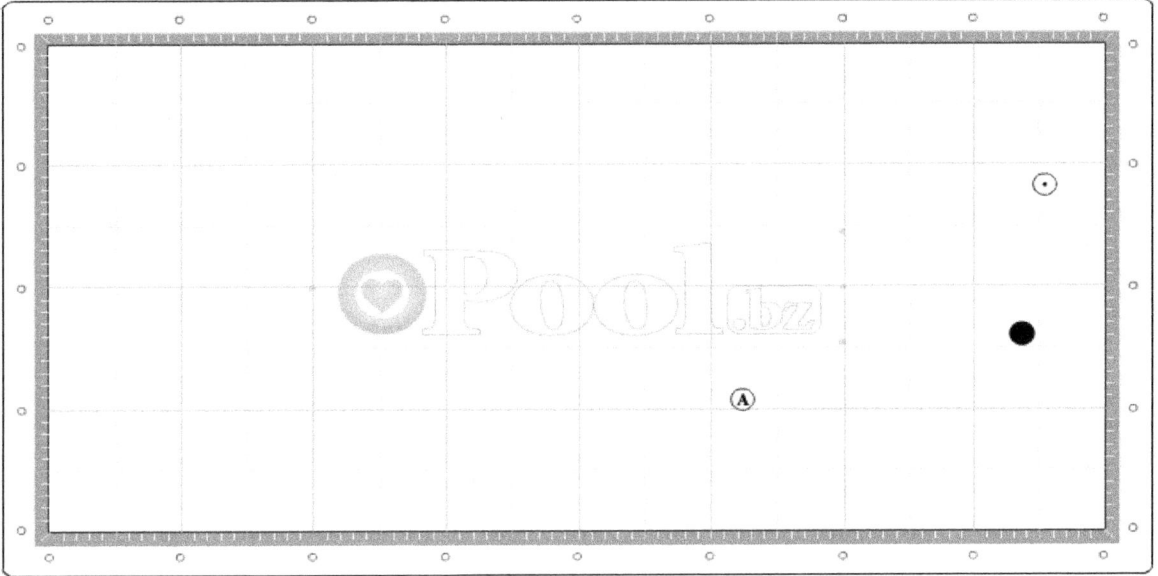

Shot Pattern

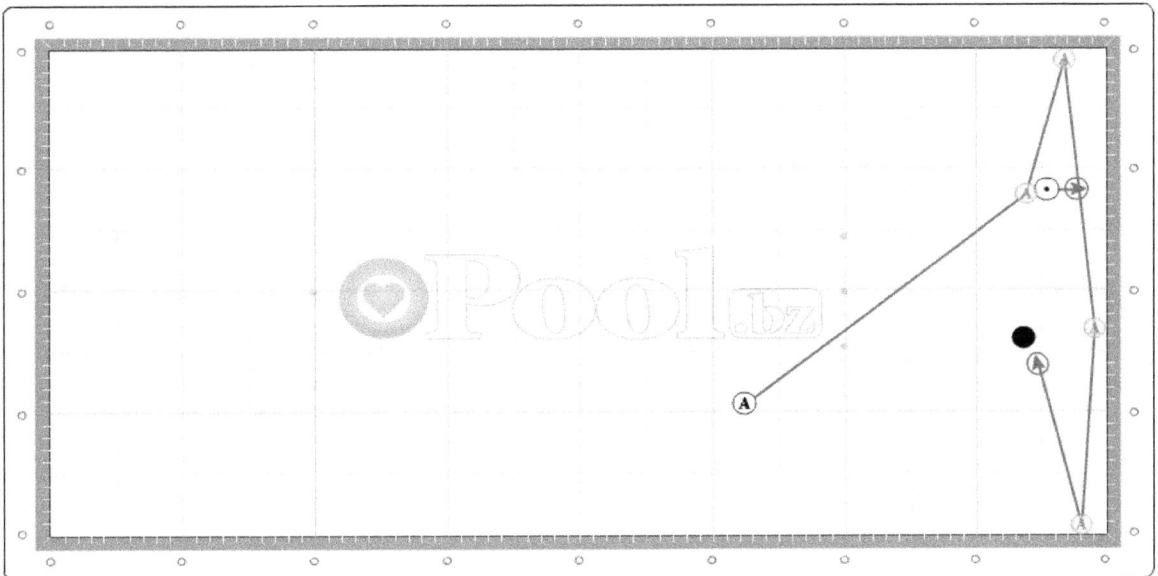

B:4d – Setup

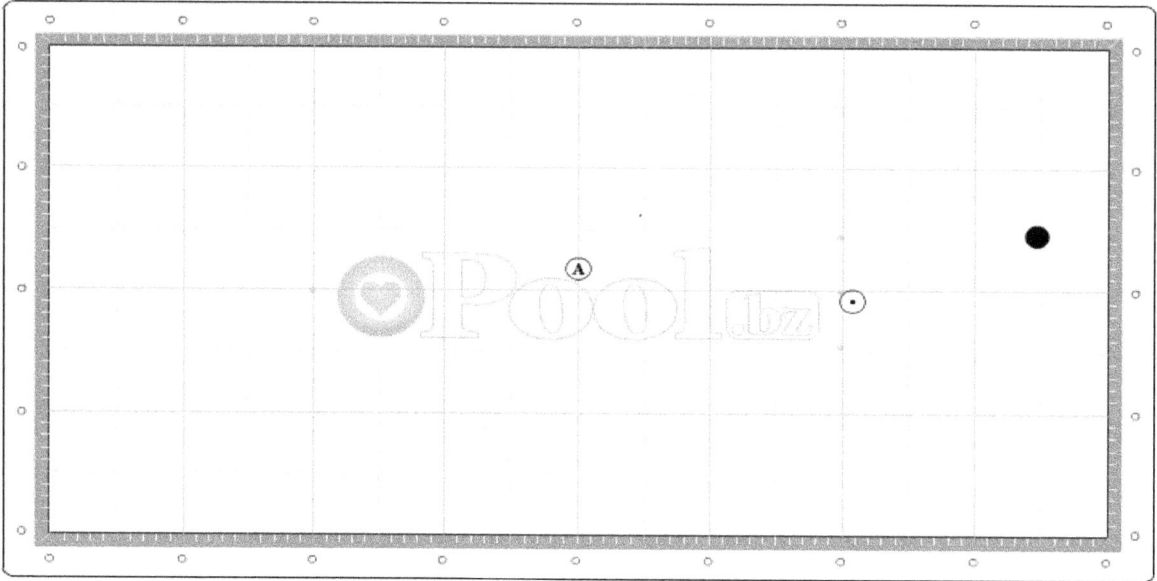

Shot Pattern

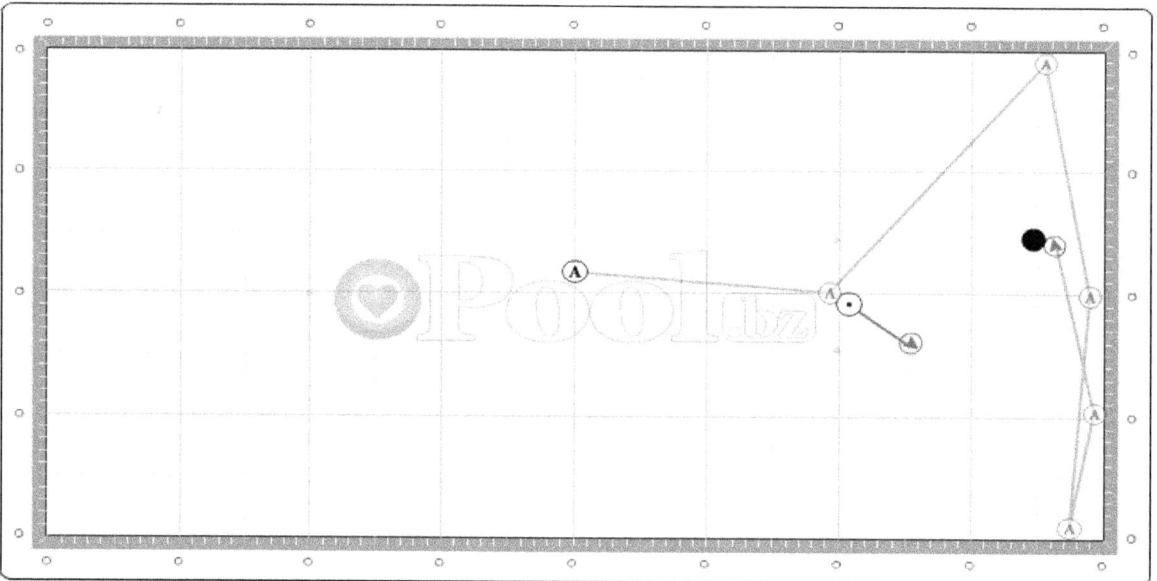

C: Ziggity-Zaggity

The CB has to travel cross table a lot. These are a lot of fun and it is worth trying these layouts.

C: Group 1

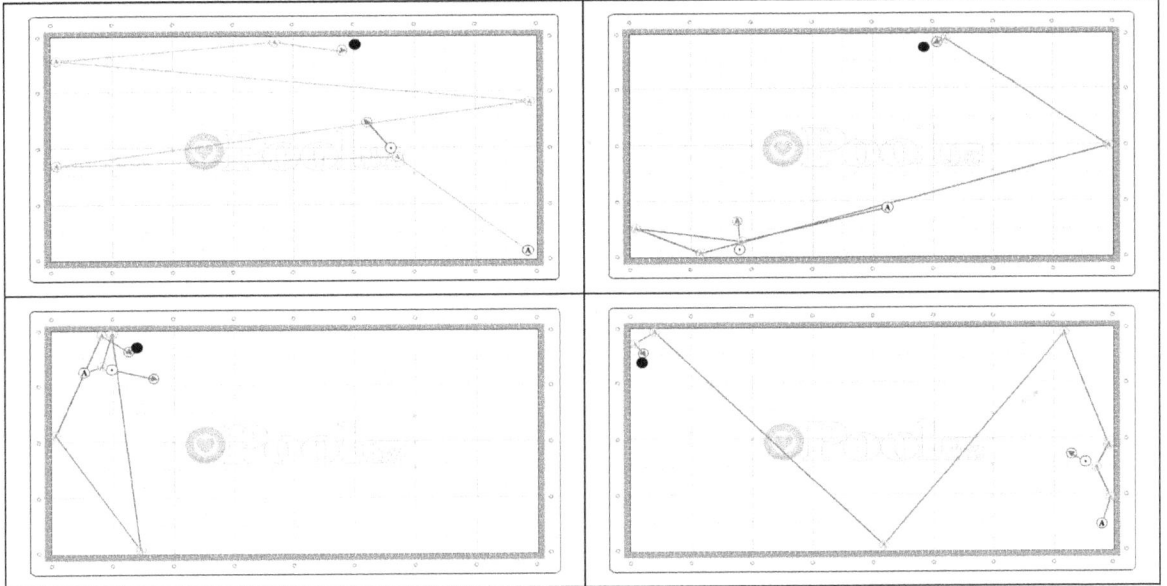

Analysis:

C:1a. _____

C:1b. _____

C:1c. _____

C:1d. _____

C:1a – Setup

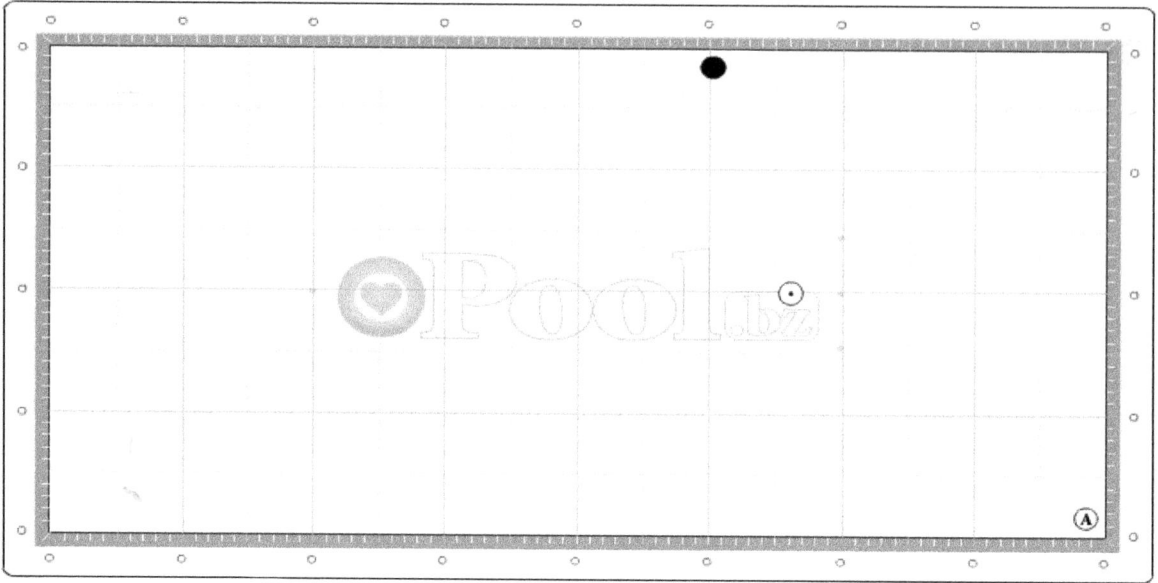

Shot Pattern

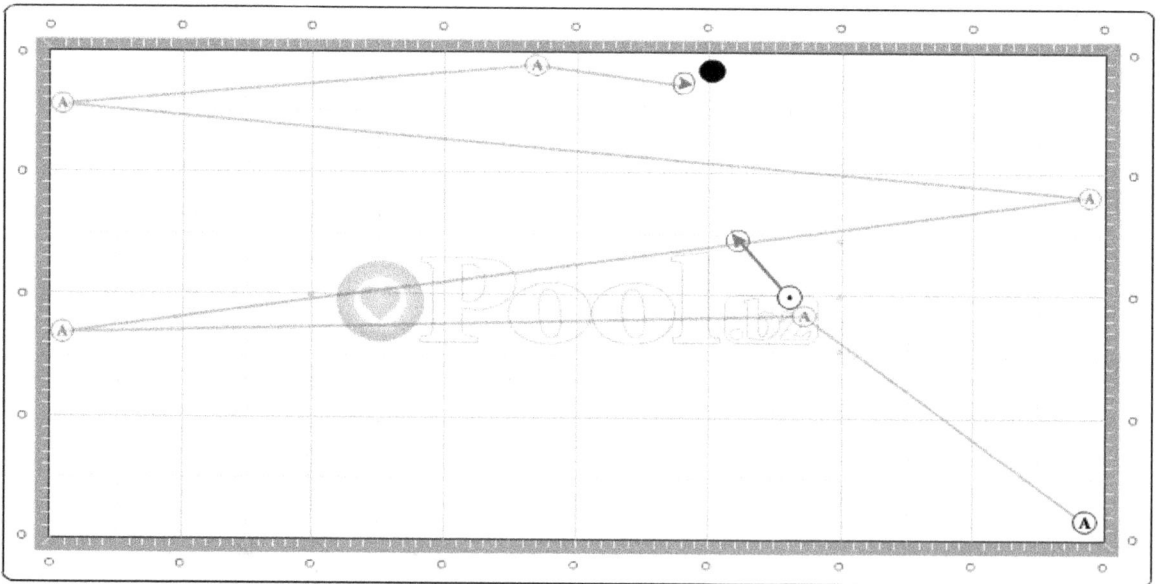

C:1b – Setup

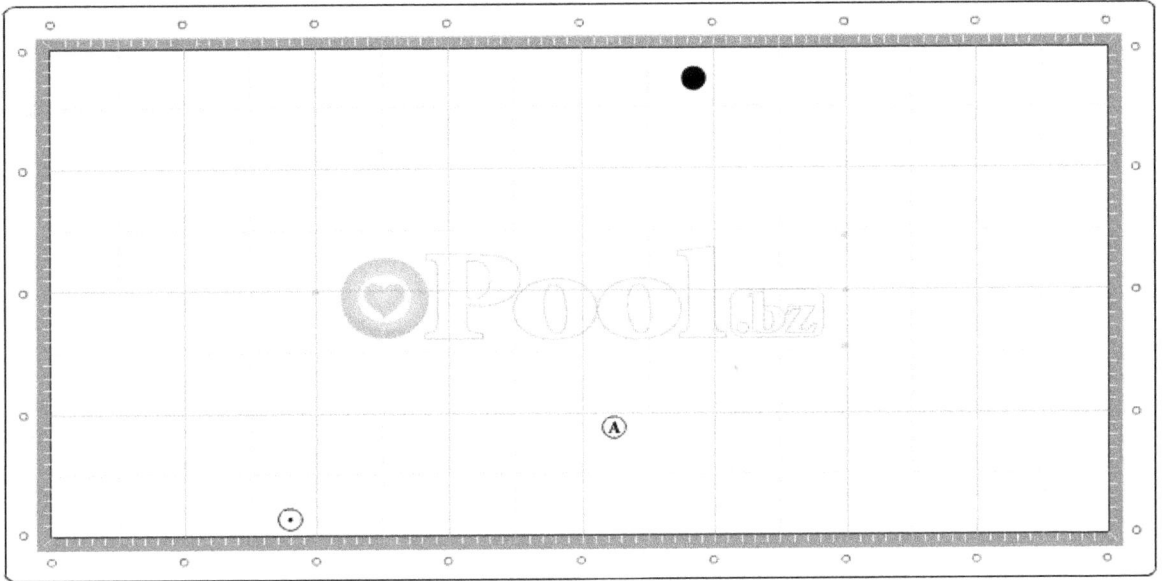

Shot Pattern

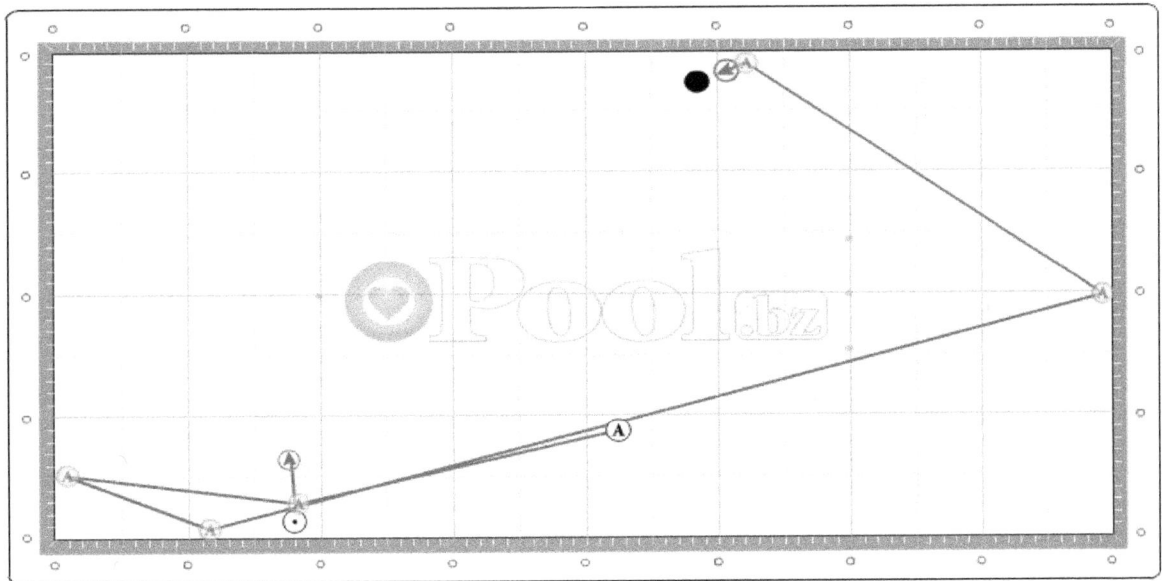

C:1c – Setup

Shot Pattern

C:1d – Setup

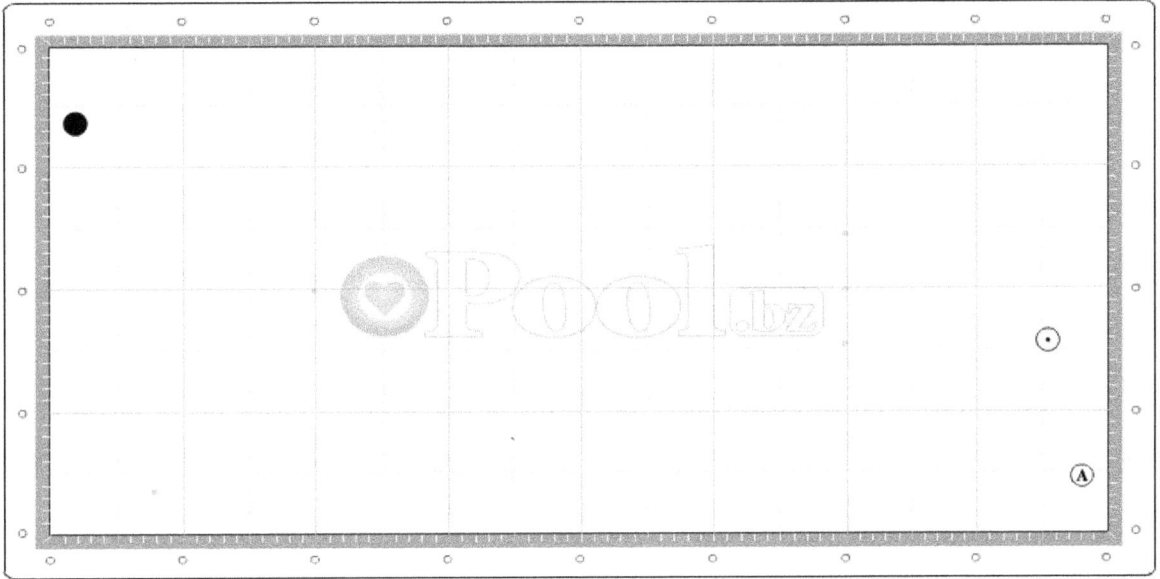

Shot Pattern

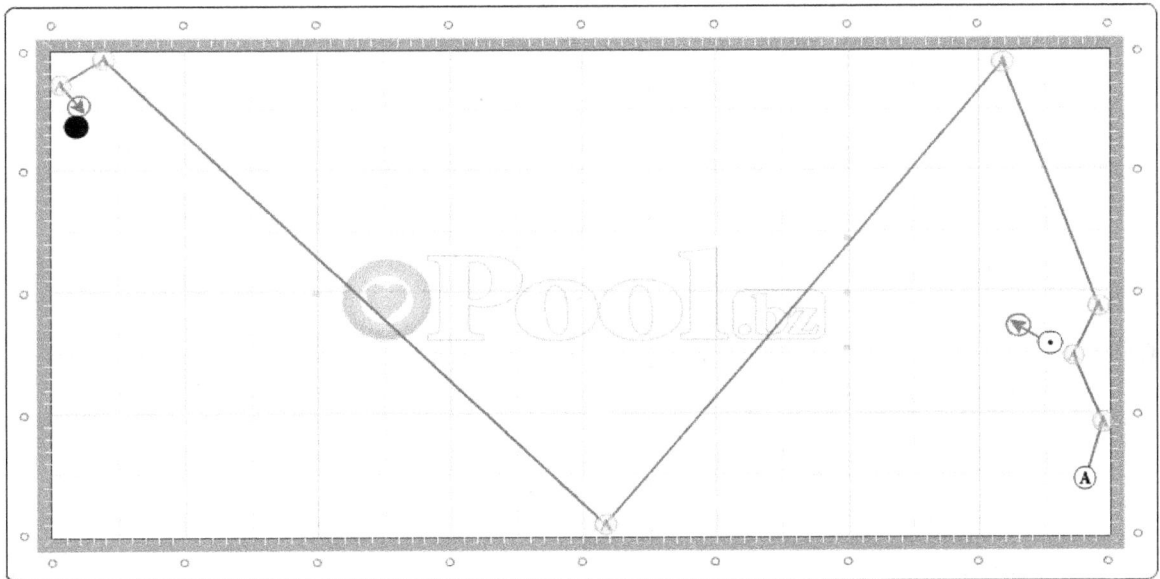

C: Group 2

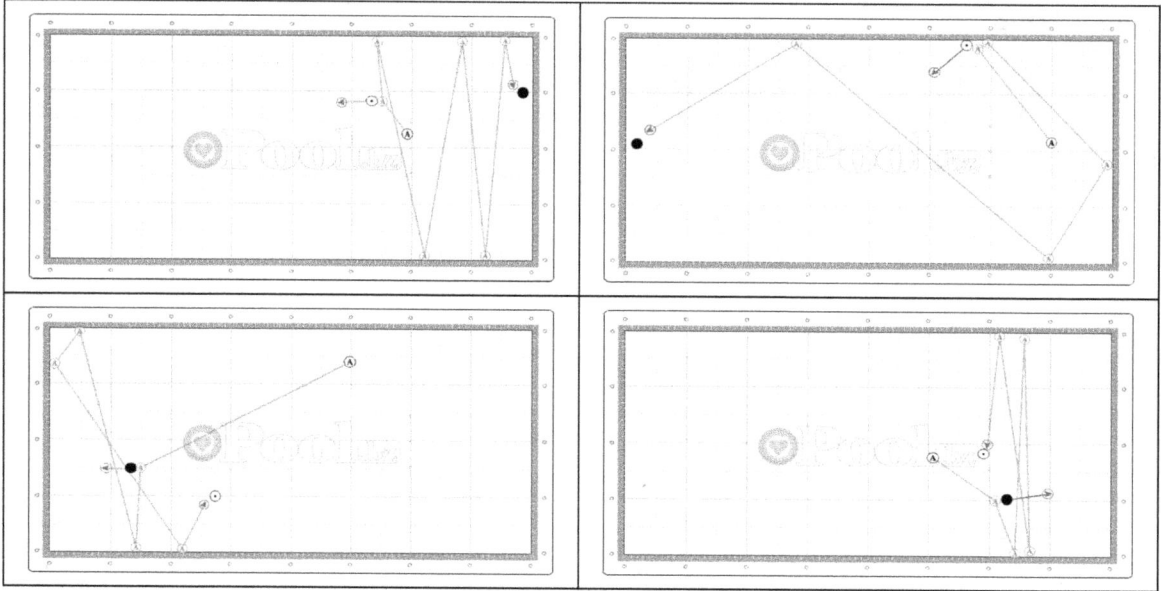

Analysis:

C:2a. _____

C:2b. _____

C:2c. _____

C:2d. _____

C:2a – Setup

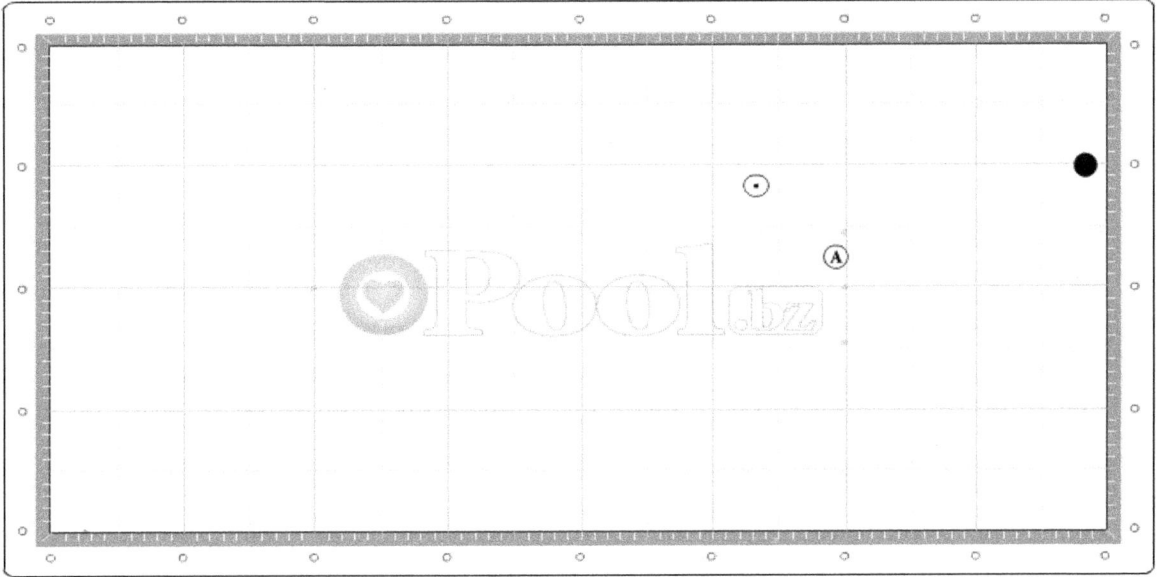

Shot Pattern

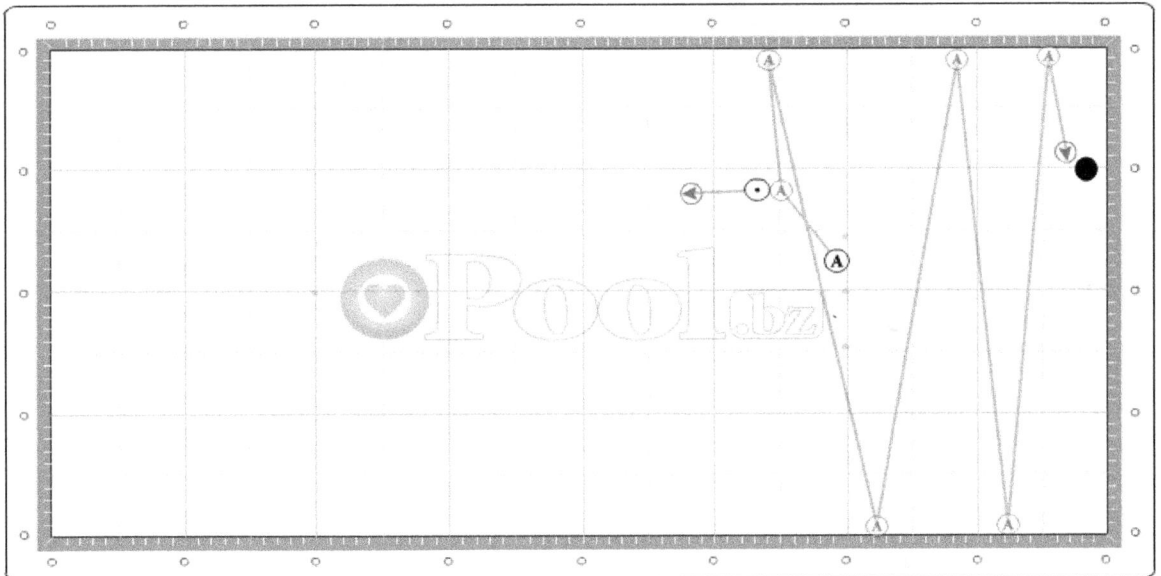

C:2b – Setup

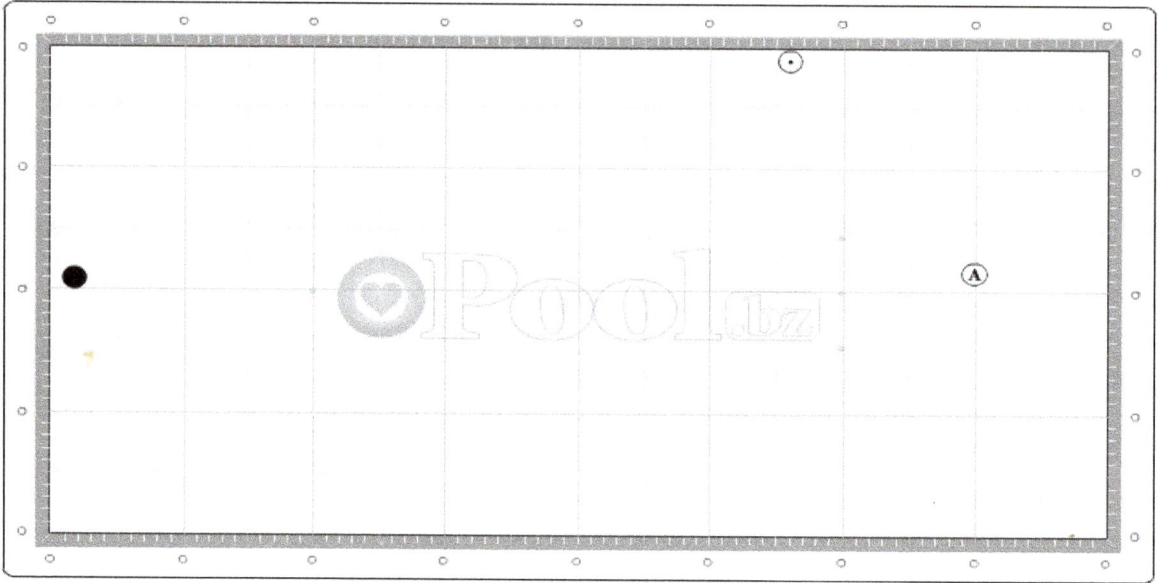

Shot Pattern

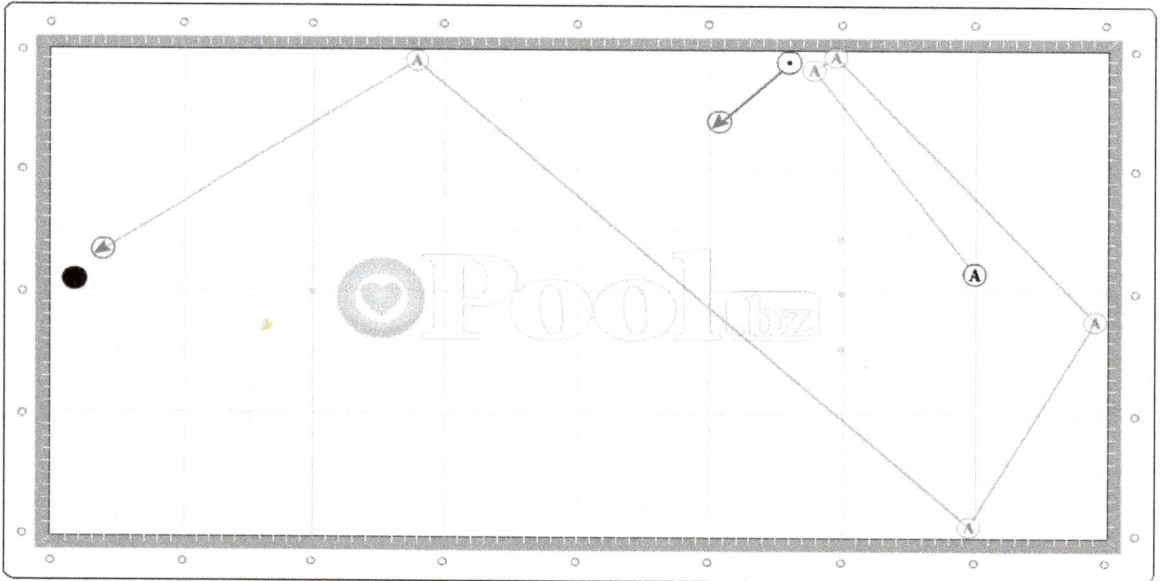

C:2c – Setup

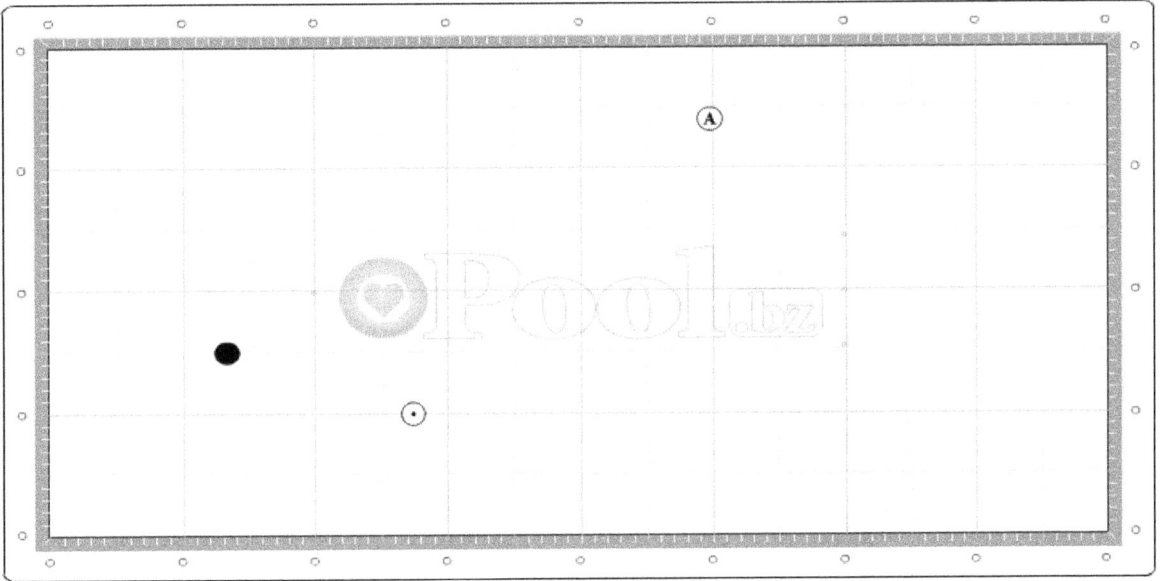

Shot Pattern

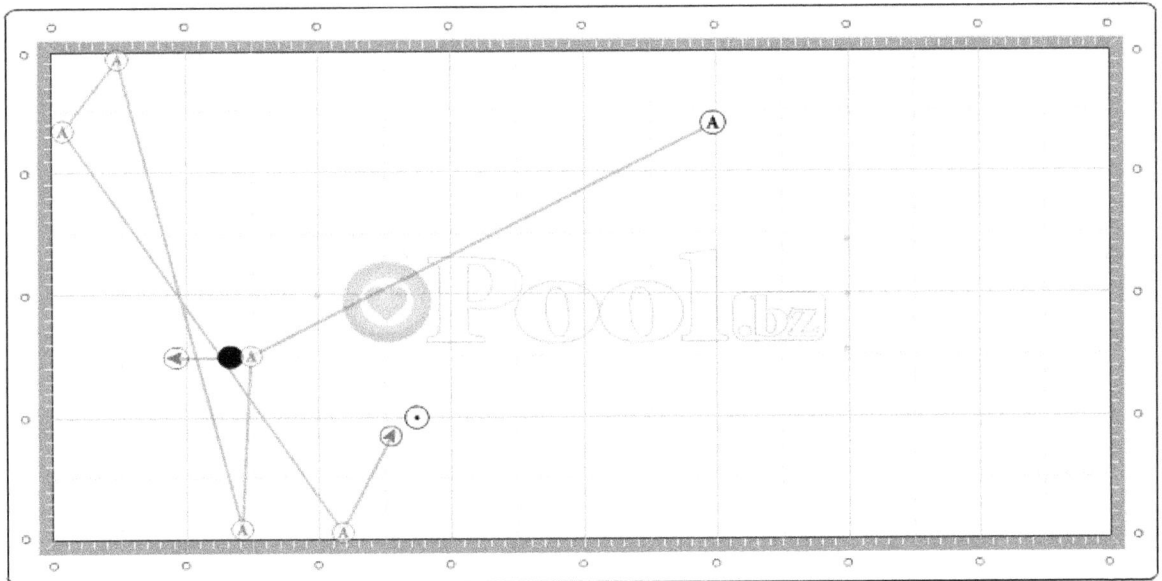

C:2d – Setup

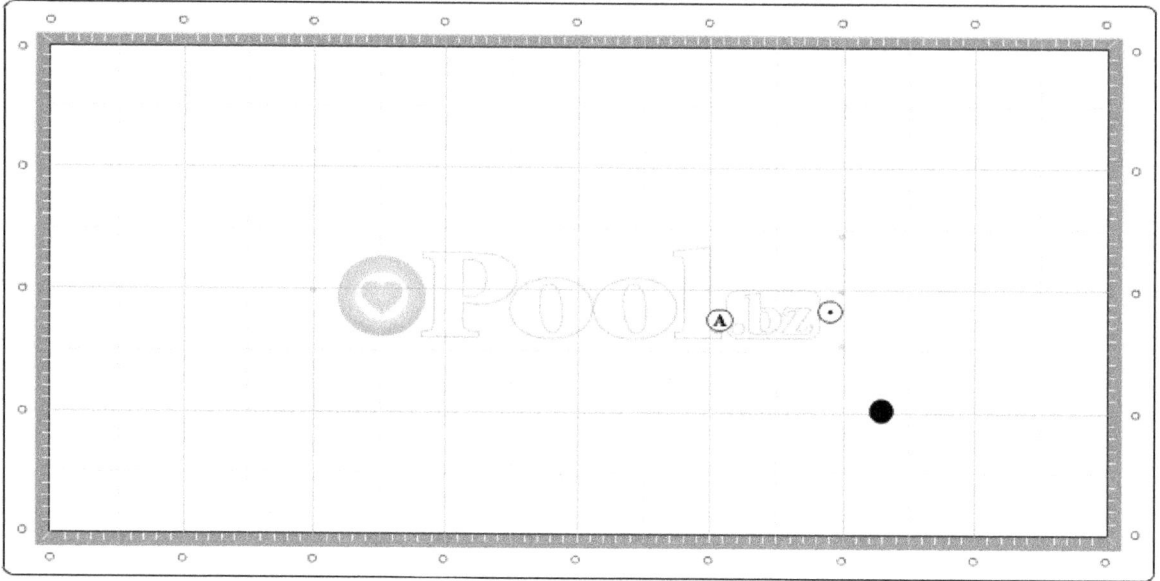

Shot Pattern

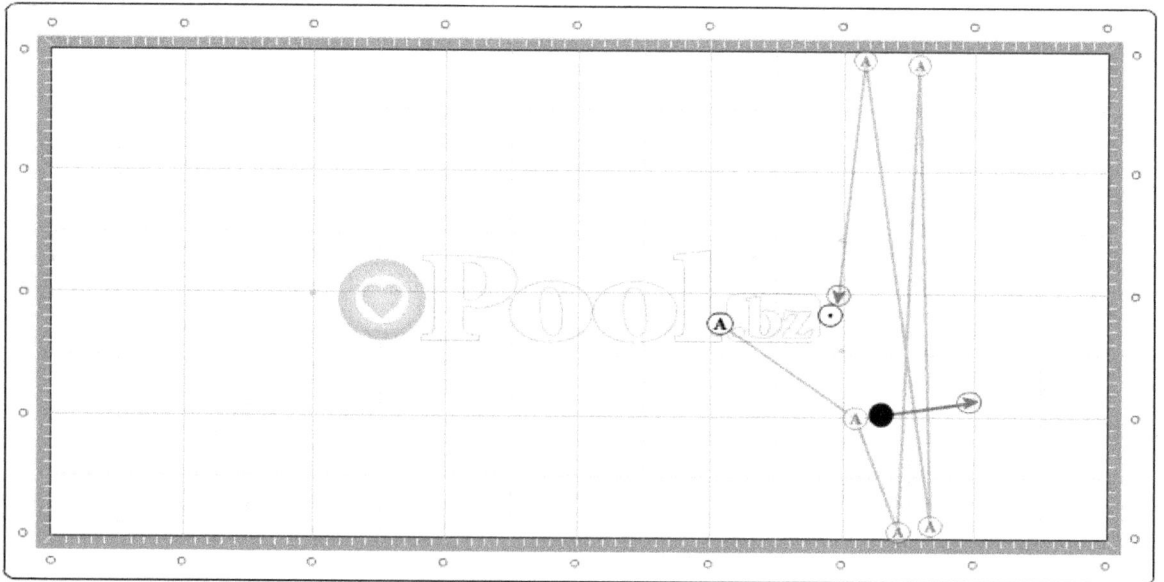

D: Lots & Lots of Rails

On these shots, the CB traveled around the table – a lot. The CB had to connect with a LOT of rails before it completed the point.

D: Group 1

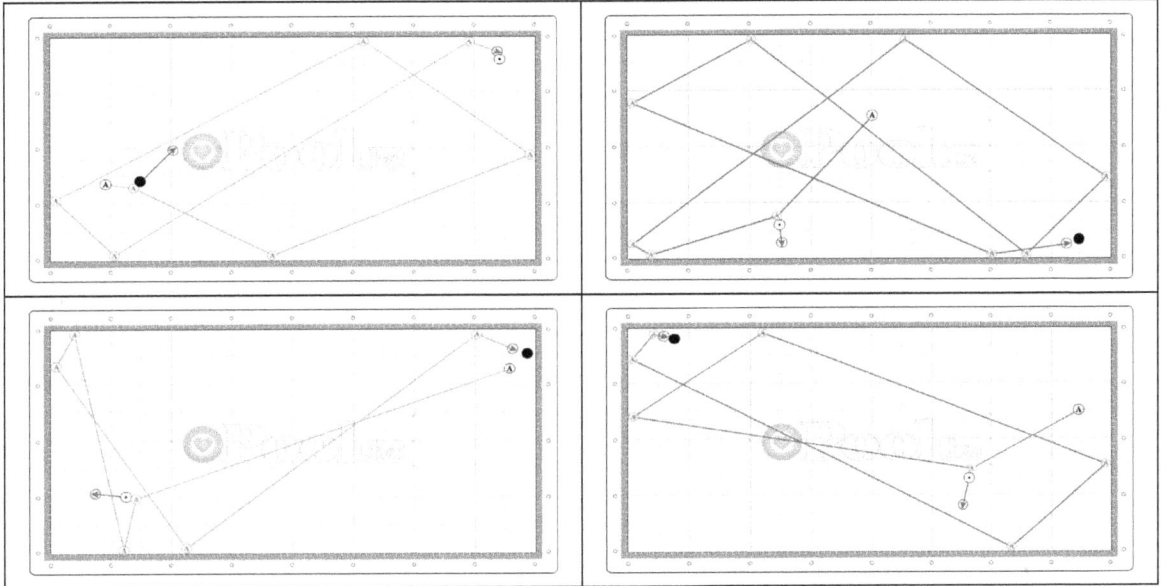

Analysis:

D:1a. _____

D:1b. _____

D:1c. _____

D:1d. _____

D:1a – Setup

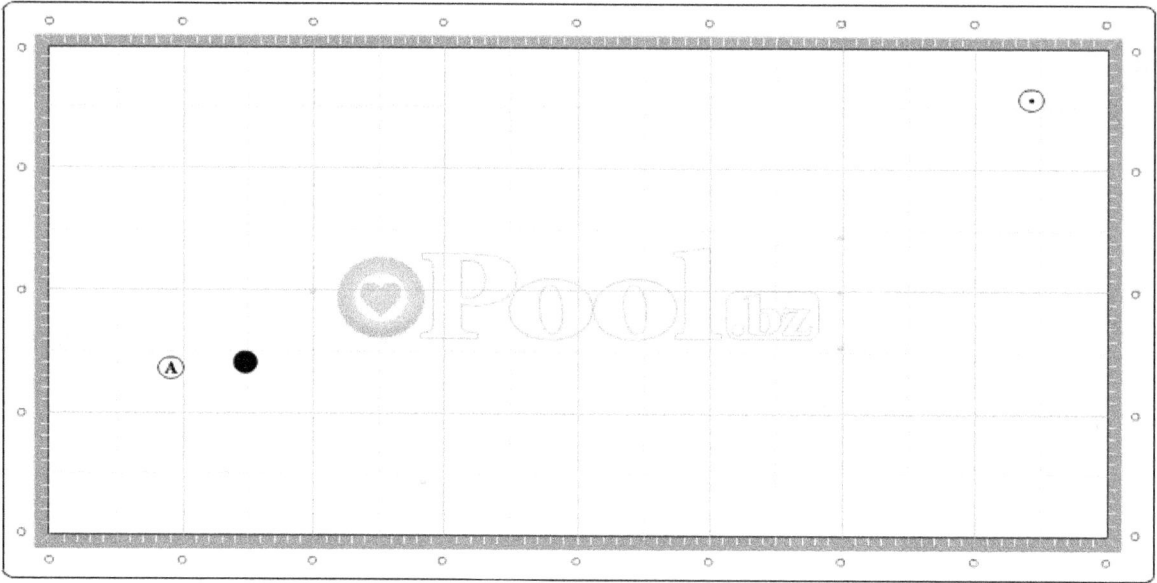

Shot Pattern

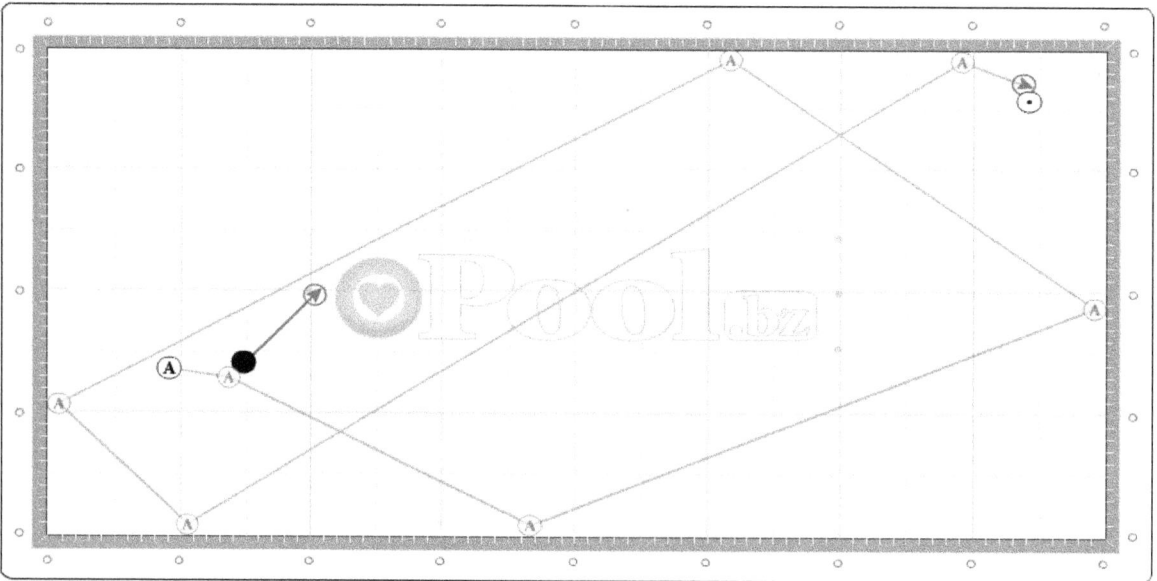

D:1b – Setup

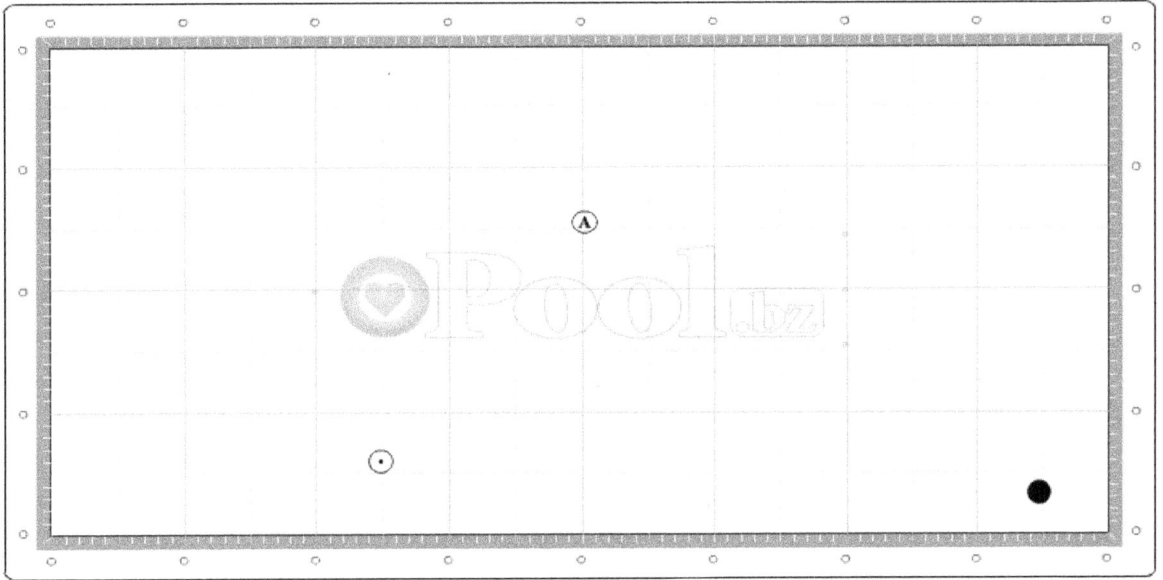

Shot Pattern

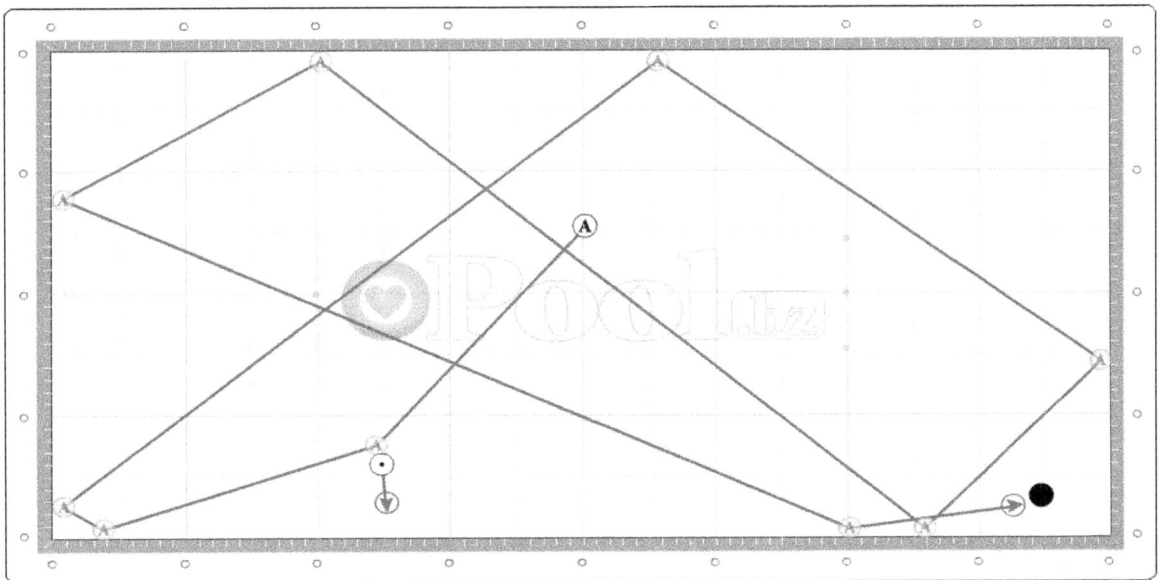

D:1c – Setup

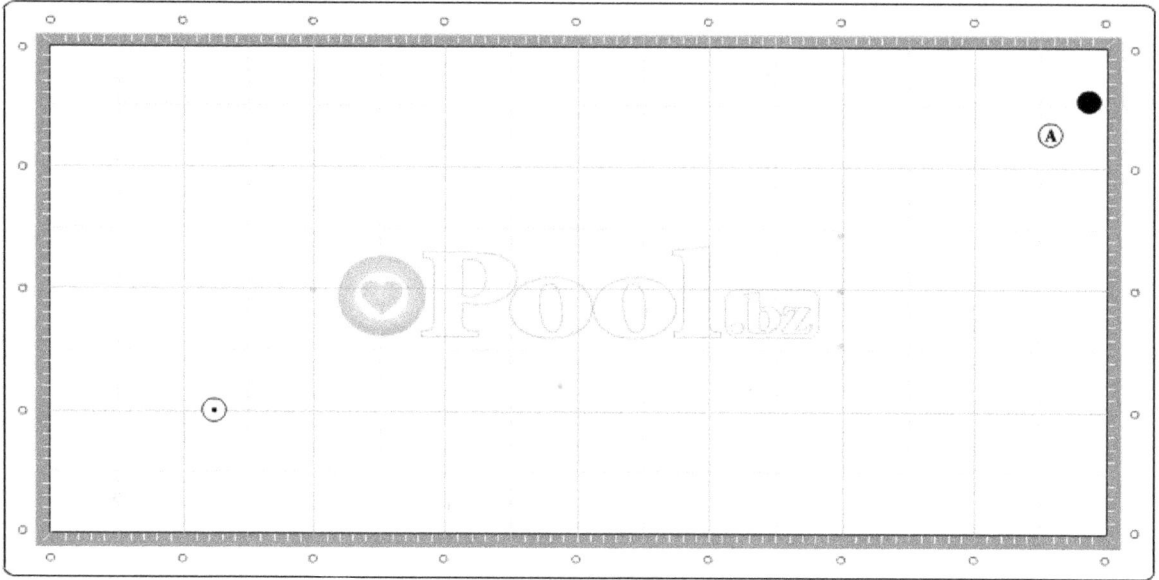

Shot Pattern

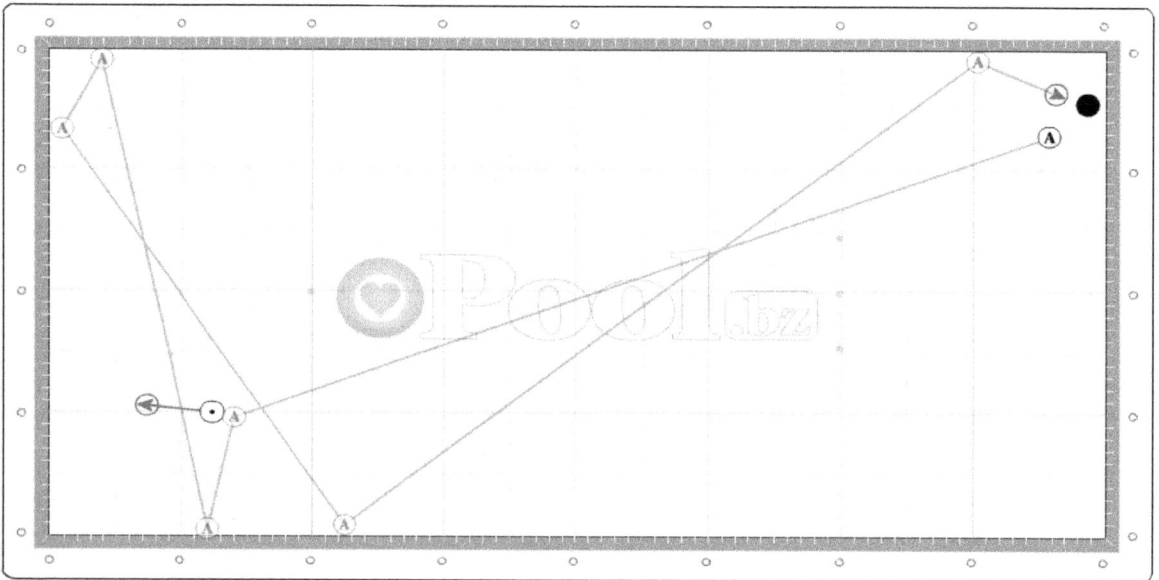

D:1d – Setup

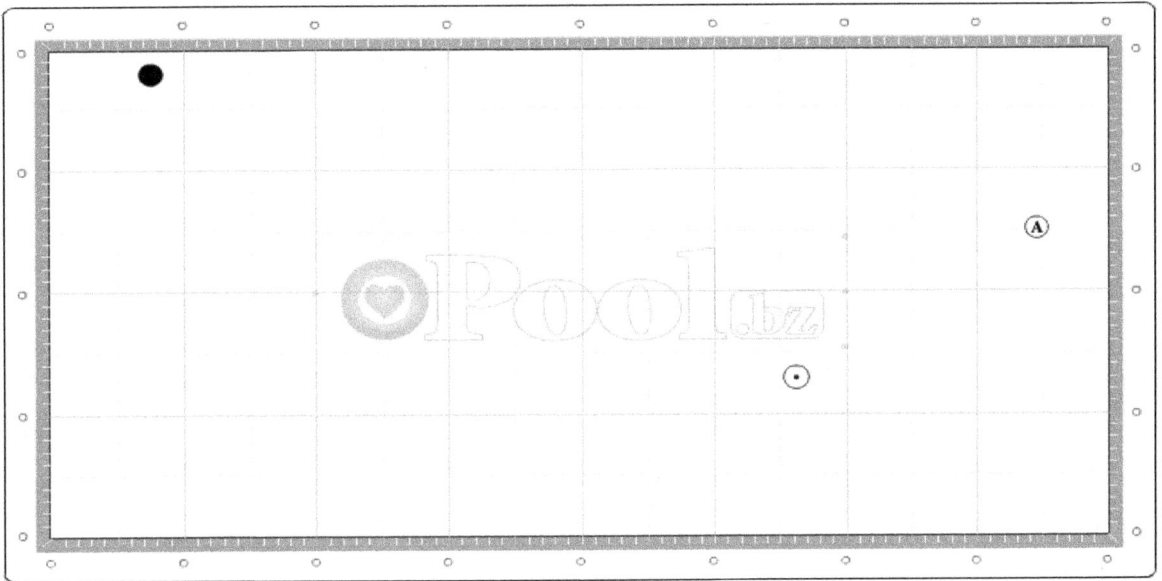

Shot Pattern

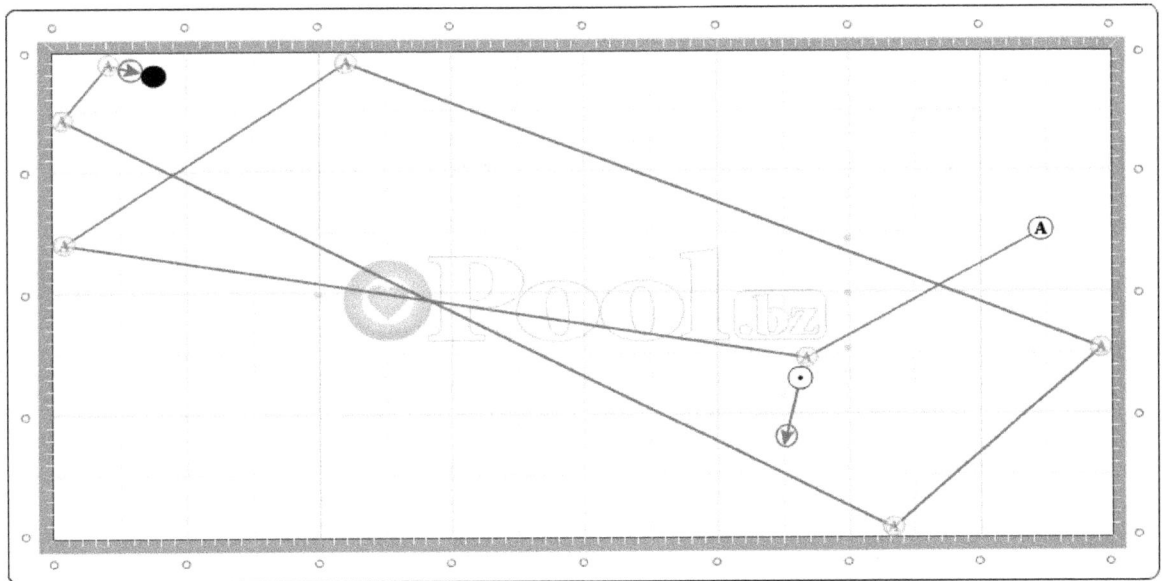

D: Group 2

Analysis:

D:2a. _____

D:2b. _____

D:2c. _____

D:2d. _____

D:2a – Setup

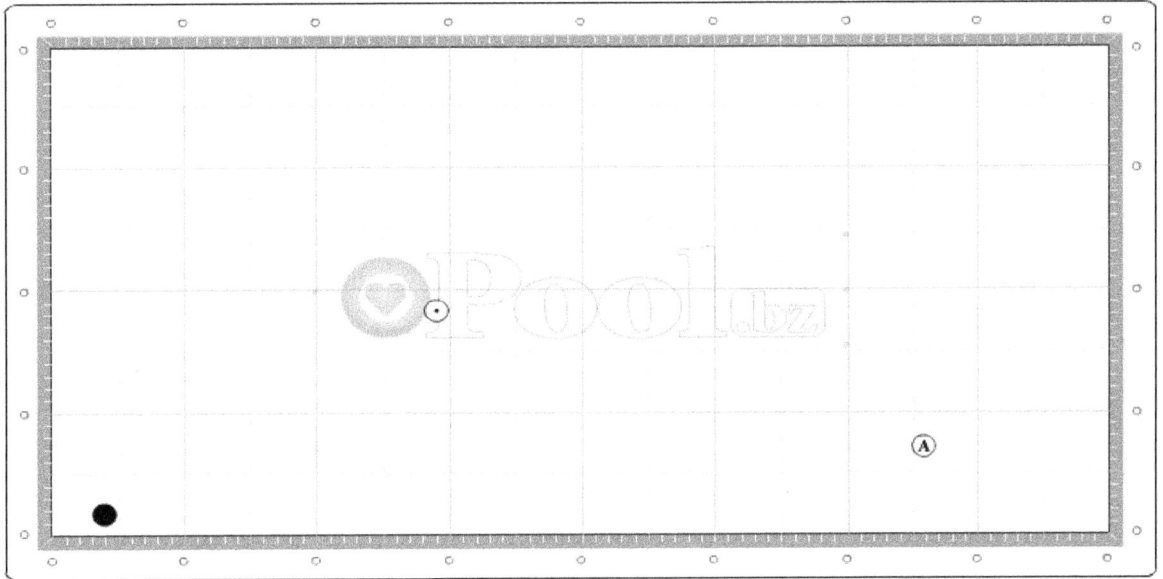

Shot Pattern

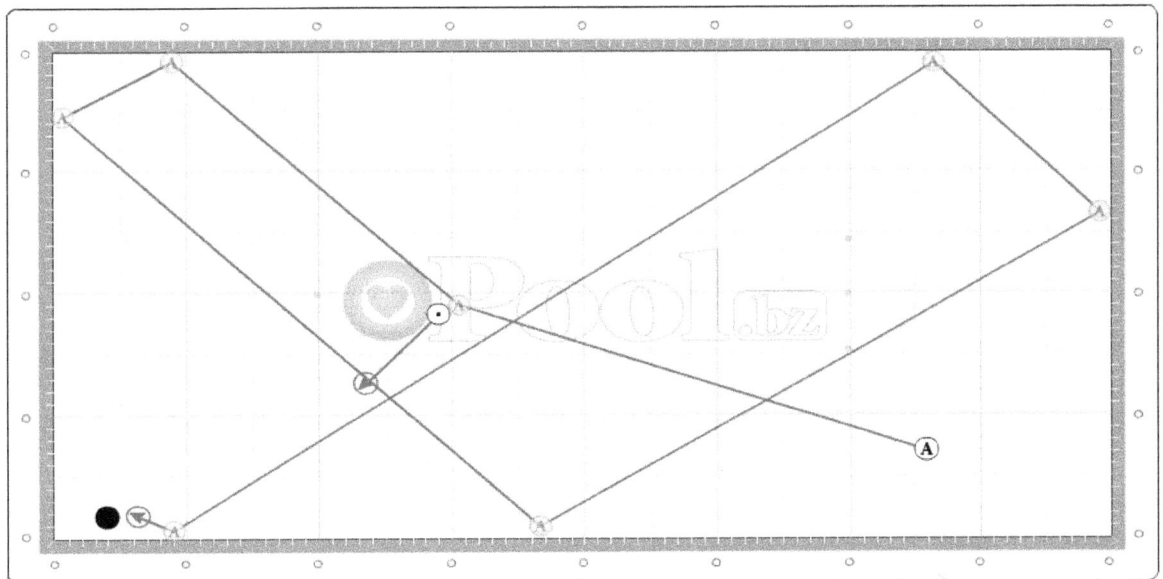

D:2b – Setup

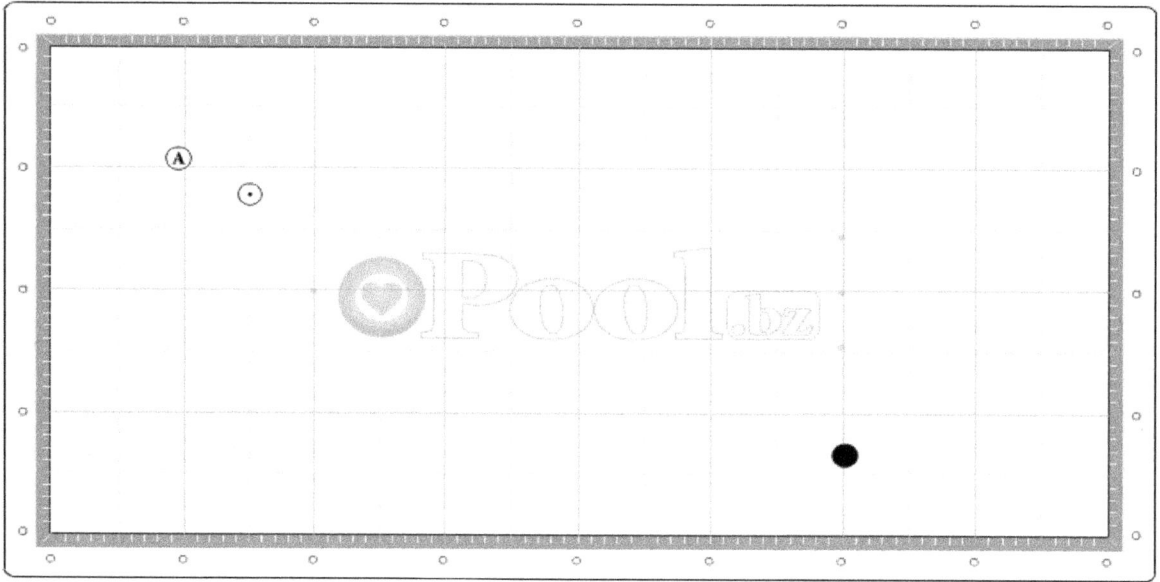

Shot Pattern

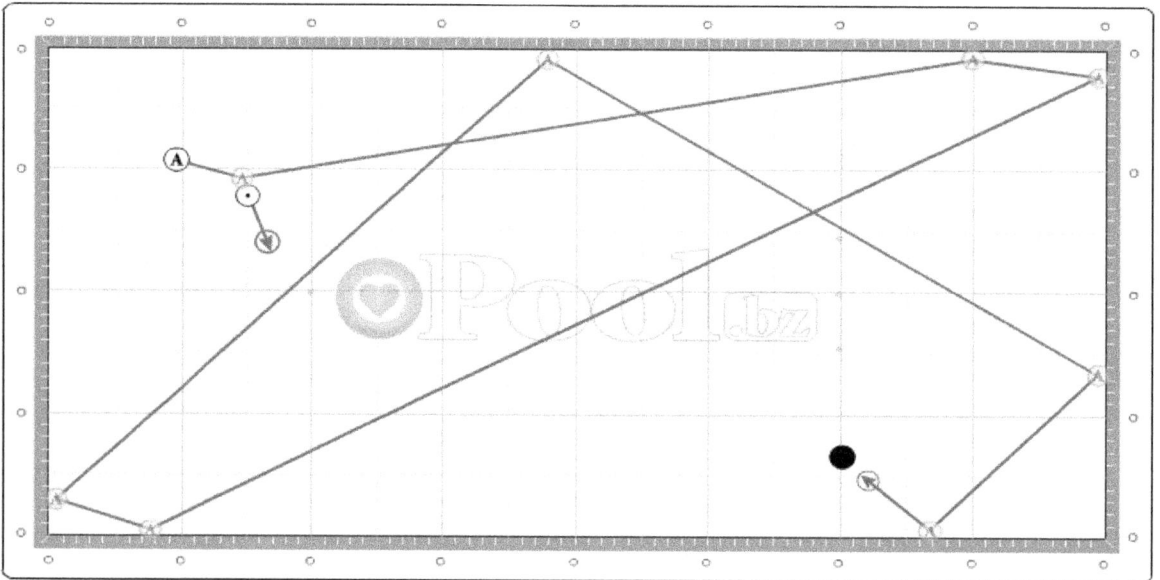

D:2c – Setup

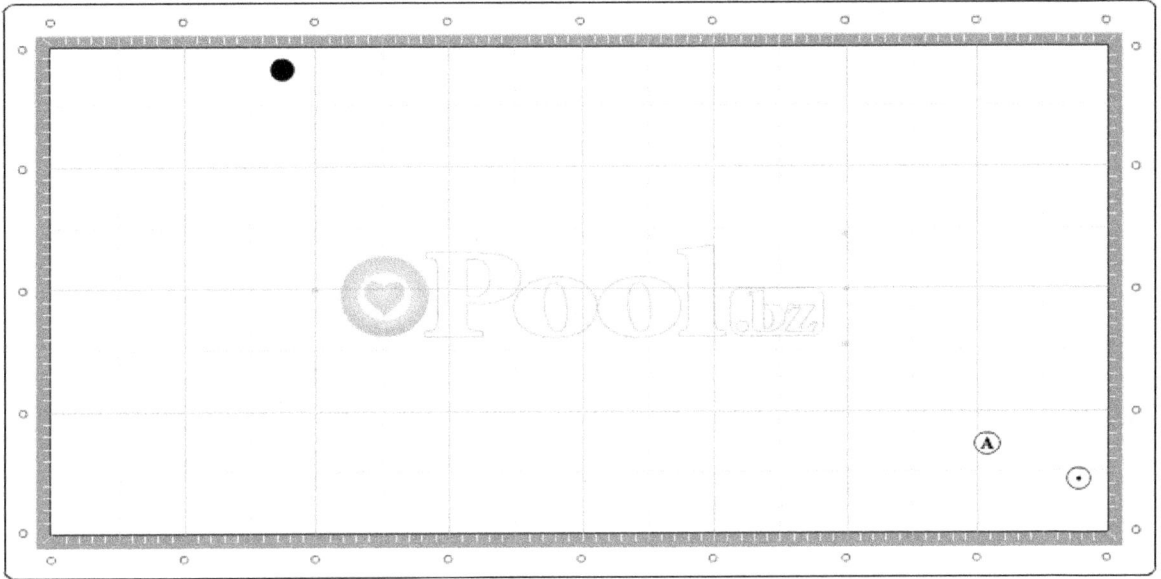

Shot Pattern

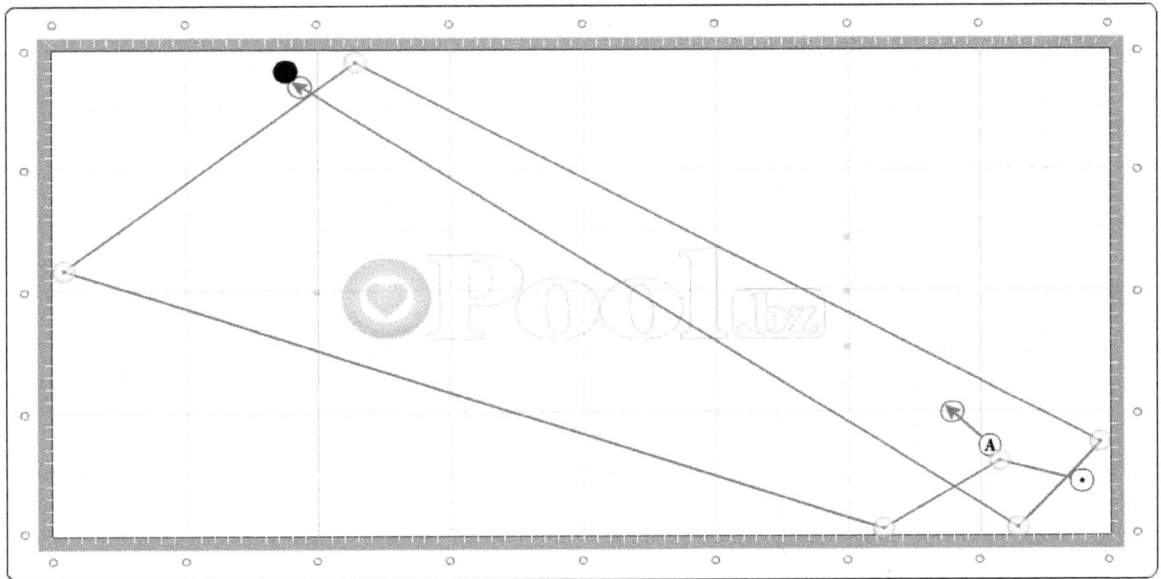

D:2d – Setup

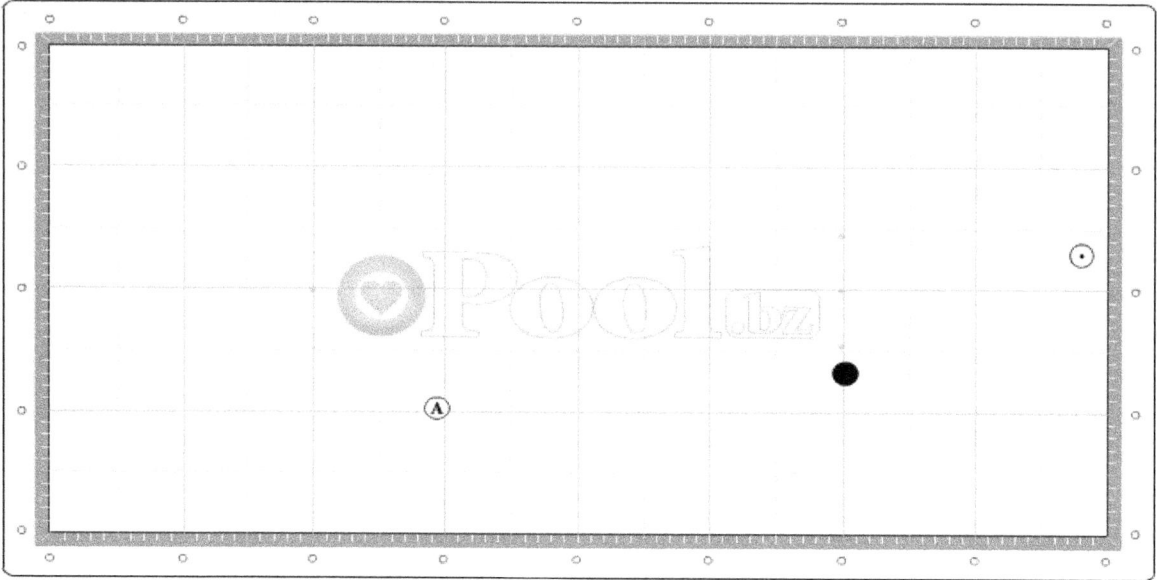

Shot Pattern

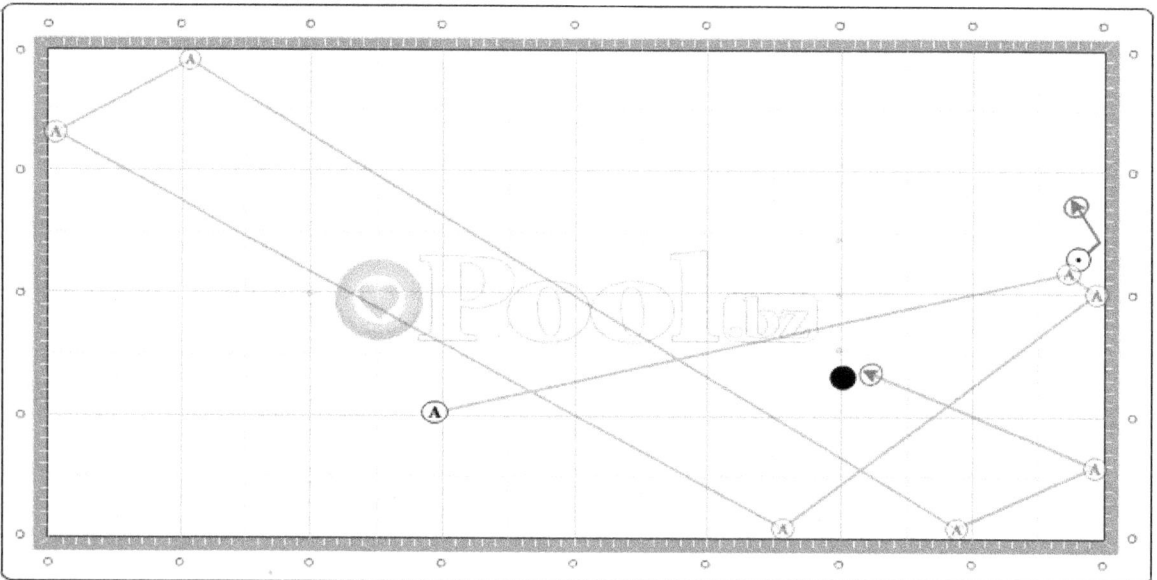

D: Group 3

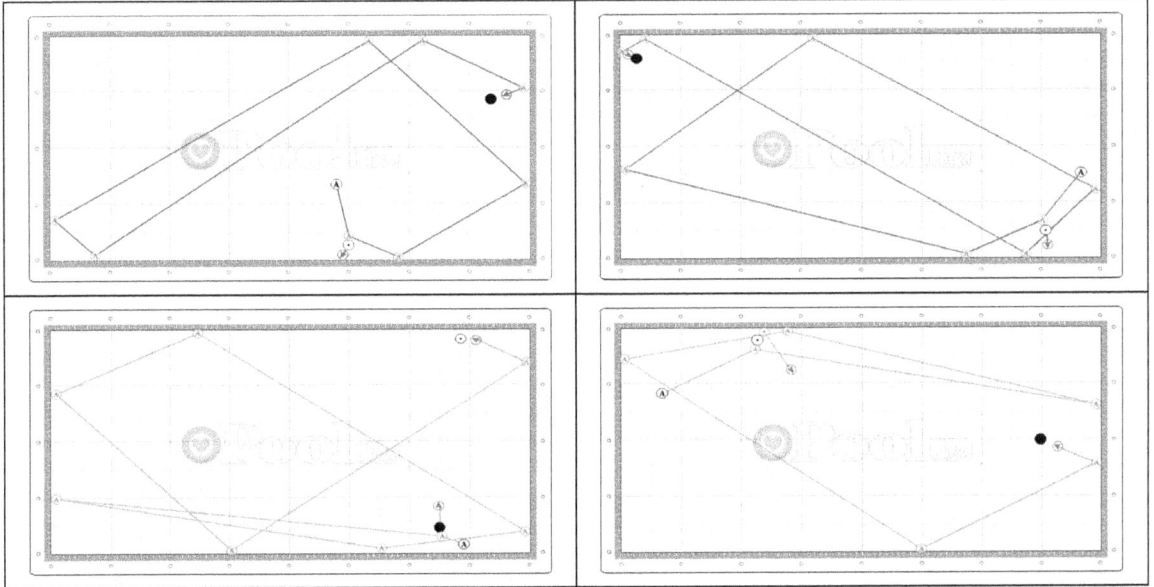

Analysis:

D:3a. _____

D:3b. _____

D:3c. _____

D:3d. _____

D:3a – Setup

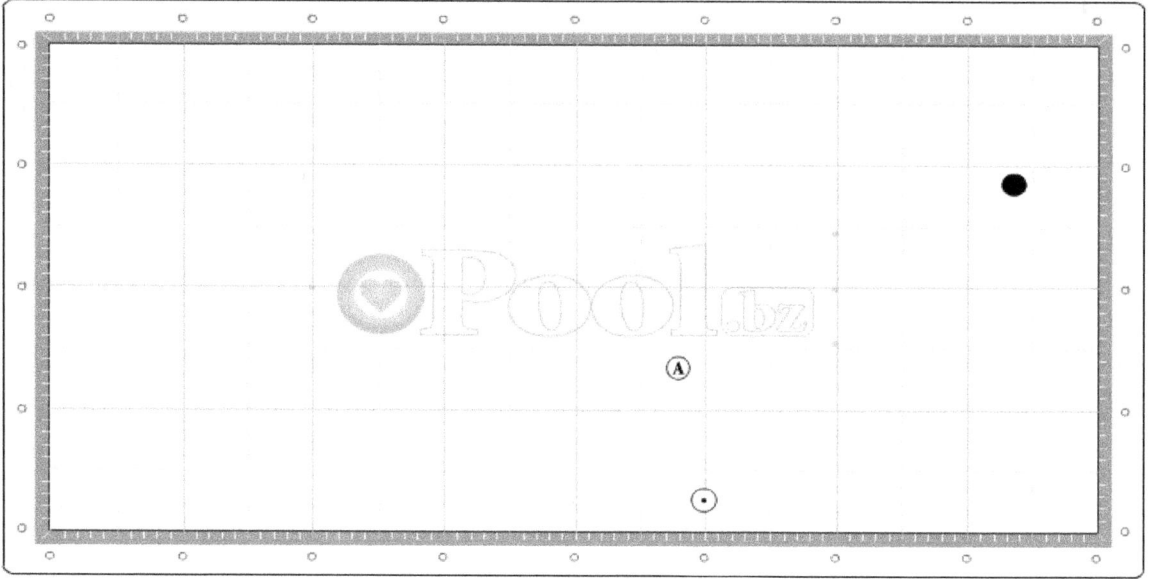

Shot Pattern

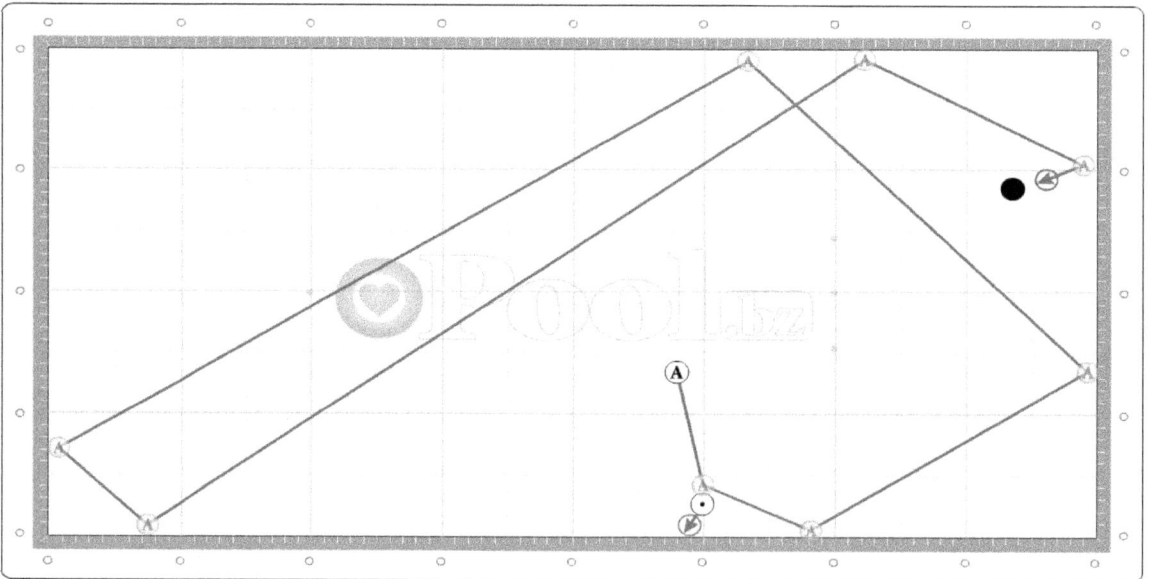

D:3b – Setup

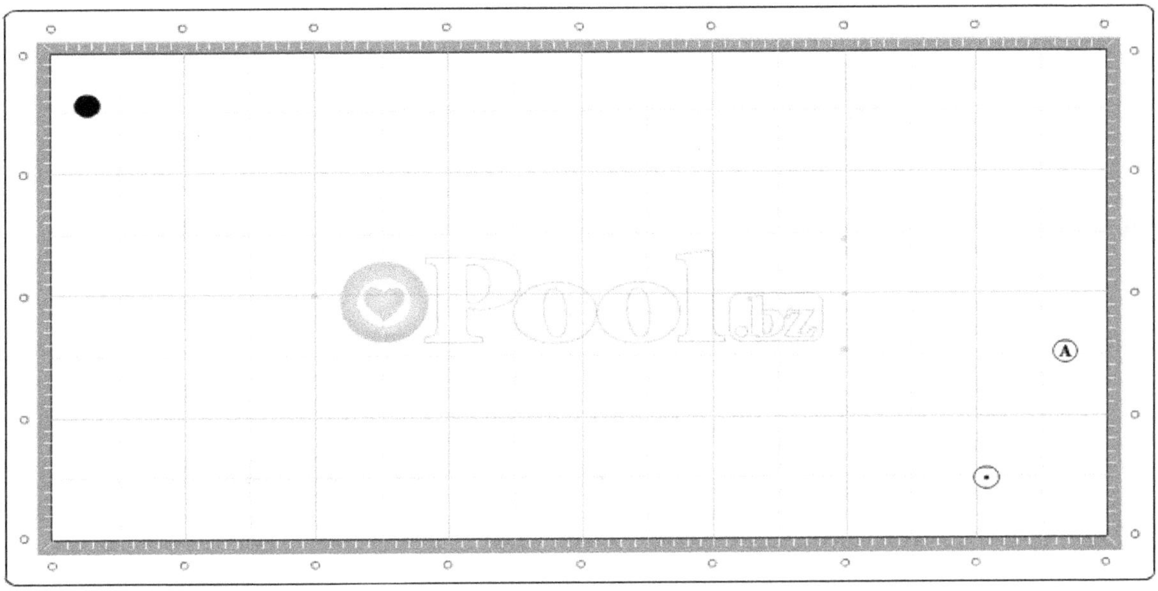

Shot Pattern

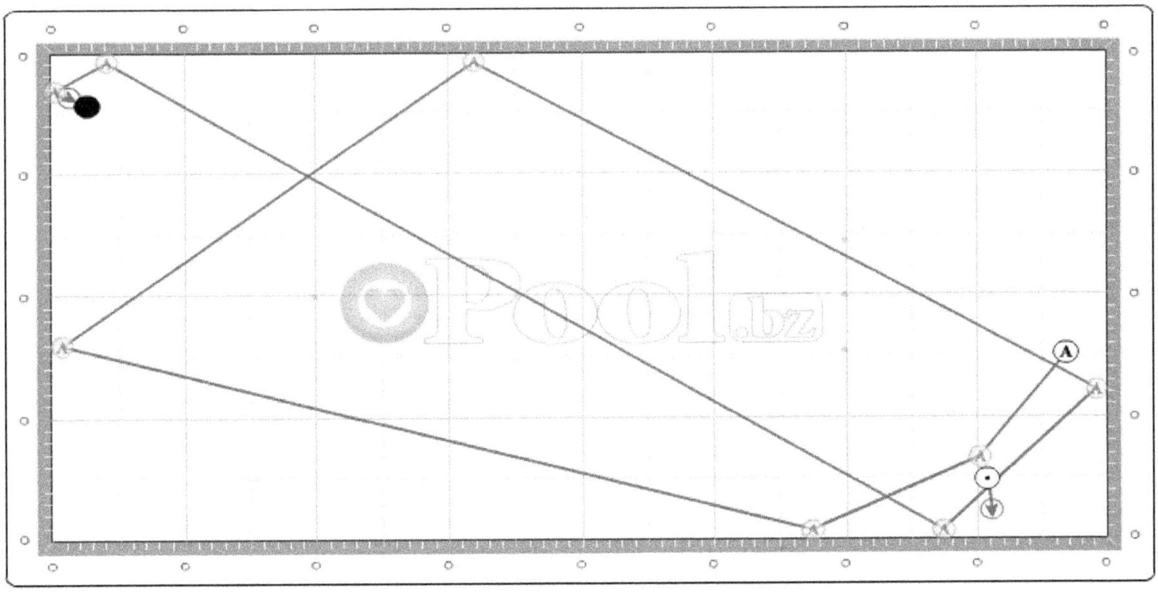

D:3c – Setup

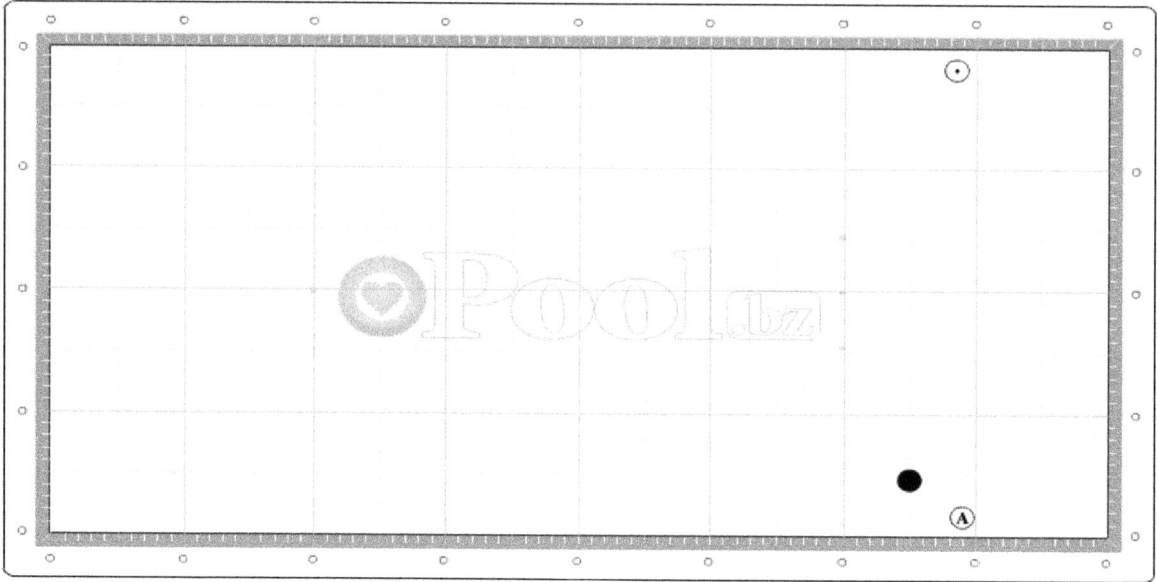

Shot Pattern

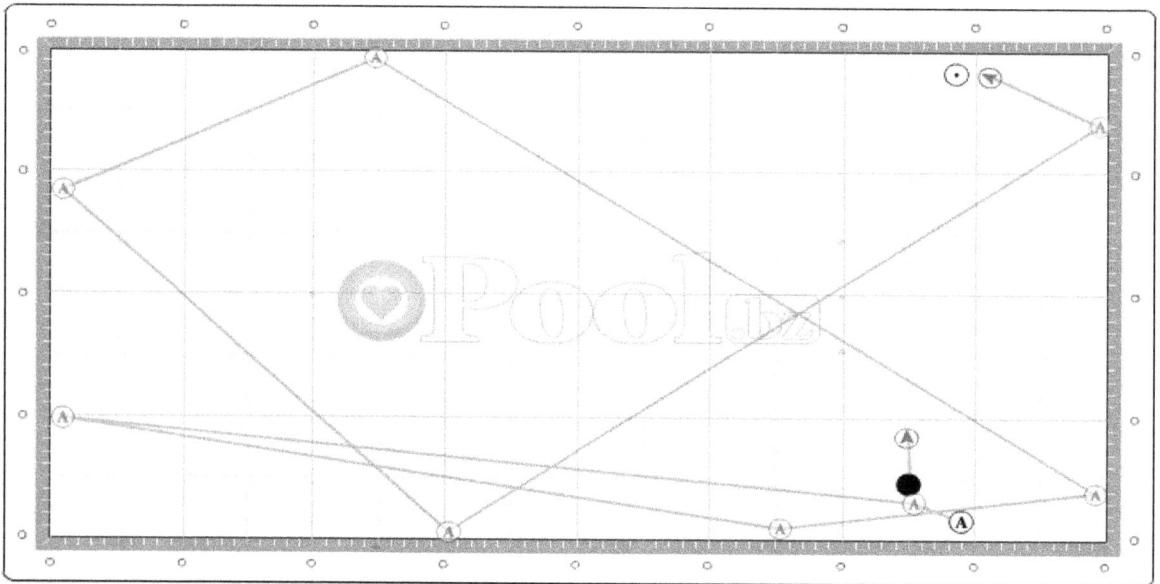

D:3d – Setup

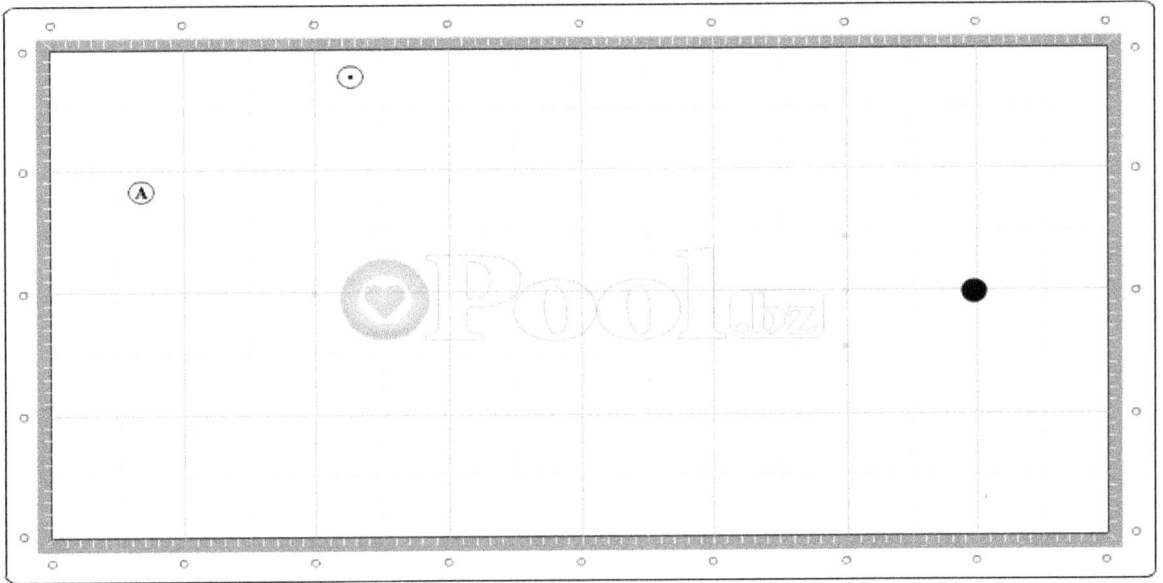

Shot Pattern

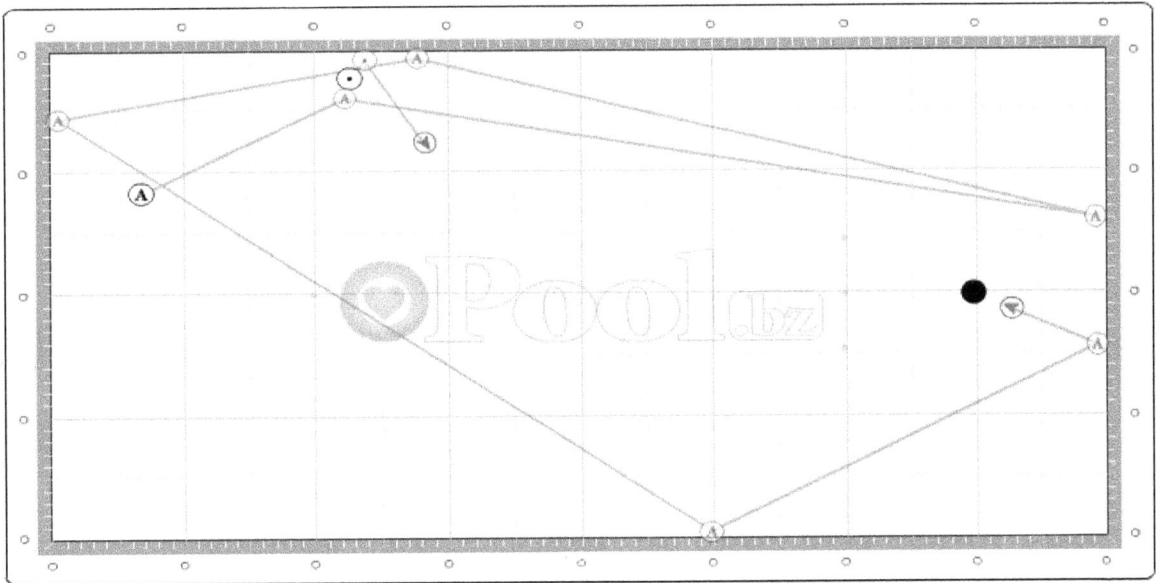

D: Group 4

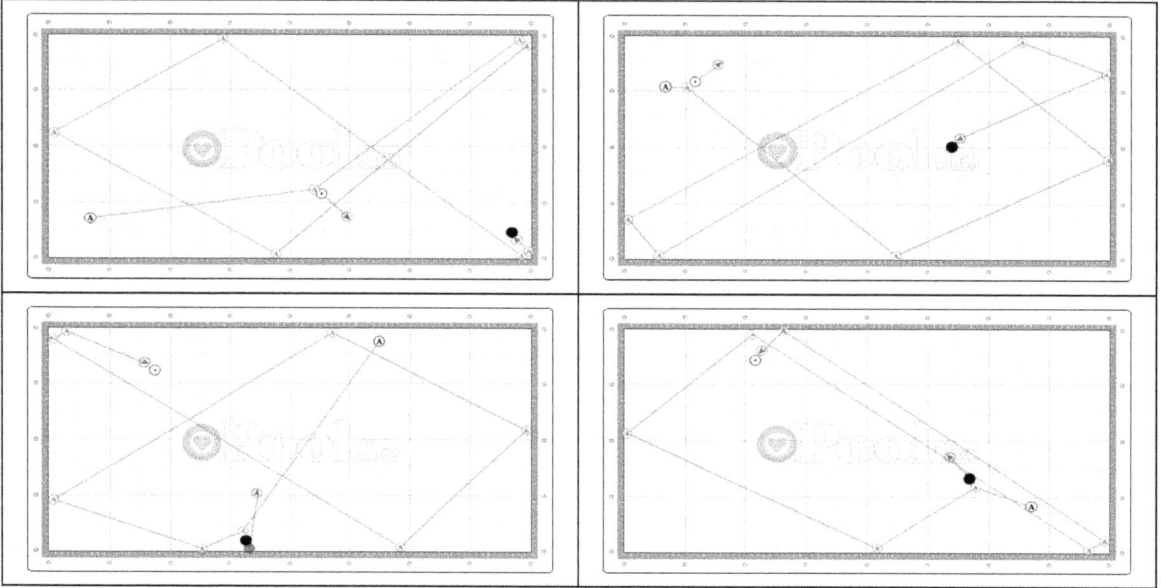

Analysis:

D:4a. _____

D:4b. _____

D:4c. _____

D:4d. _____

D:4a – Setup

Shot Pattern

D:4b – Setup

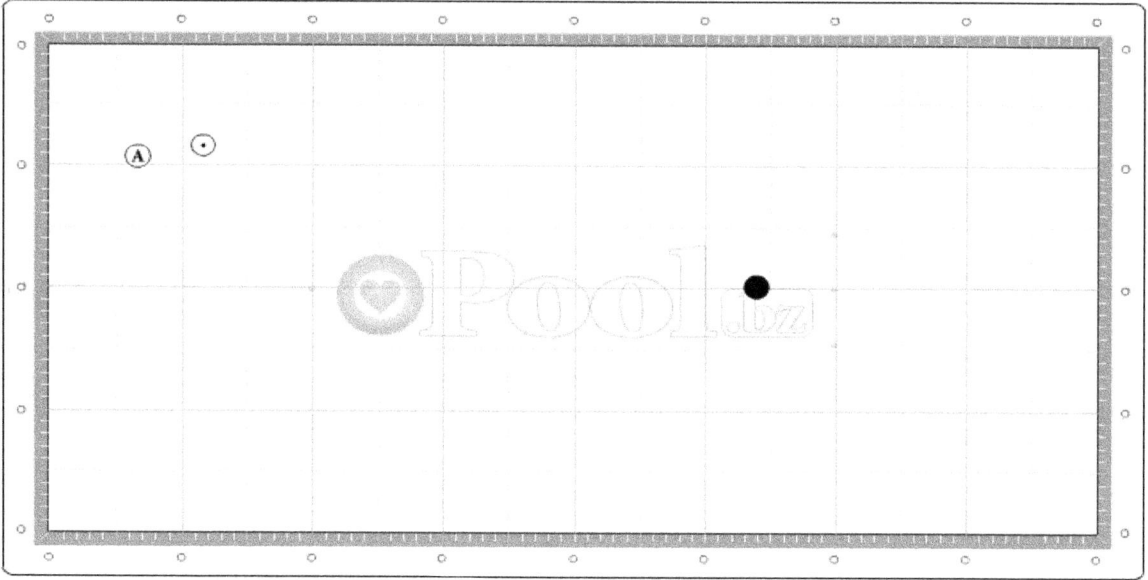

Shot Pattern

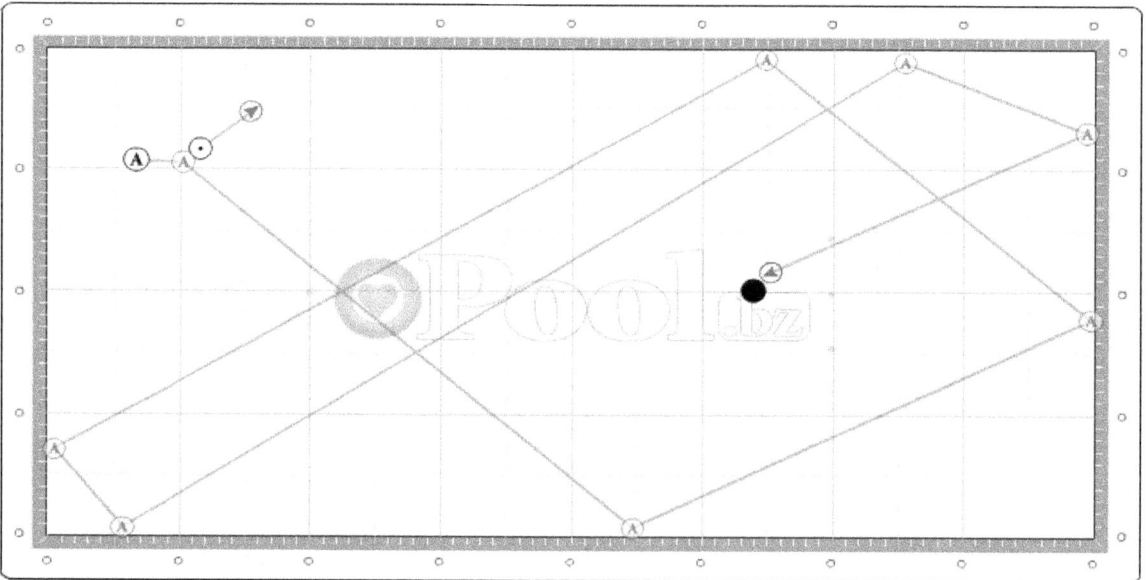

D:4c – Setup

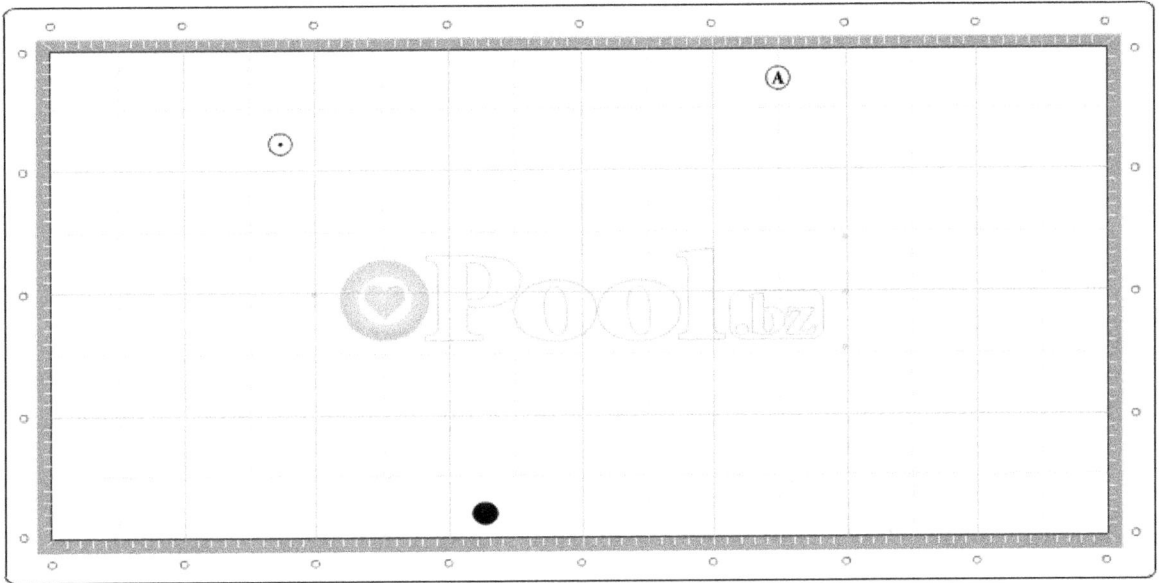

Shot Pattern

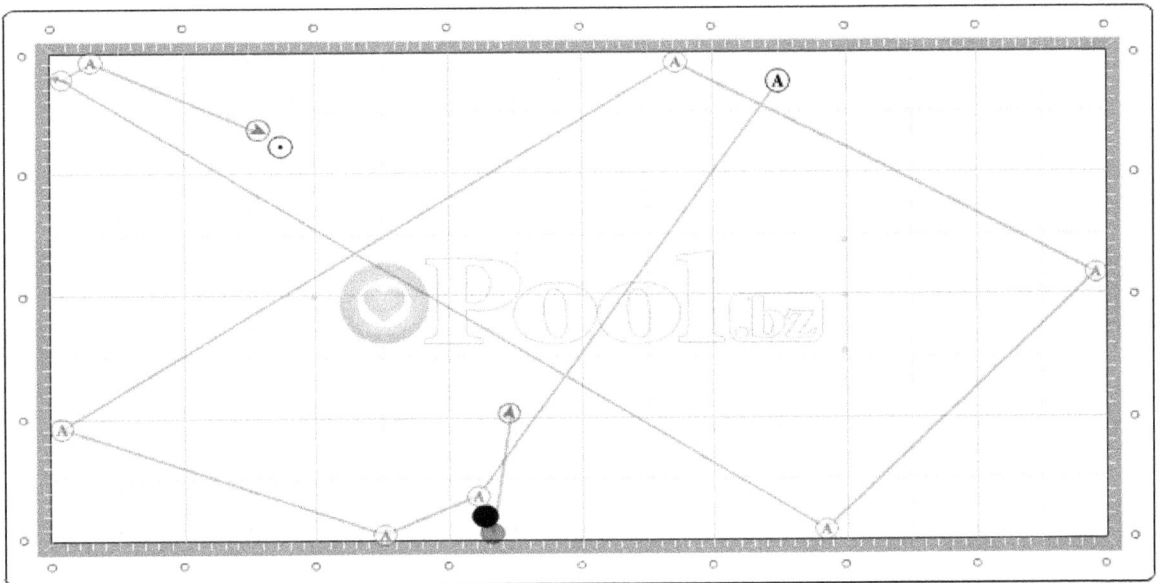

D:4d – Setup

Shot Pattern

E: Parallel Patterns

These shots sent the CB into the corner. The CB came out of the corner on a parallel line to the path into the corner.

E: Group 1

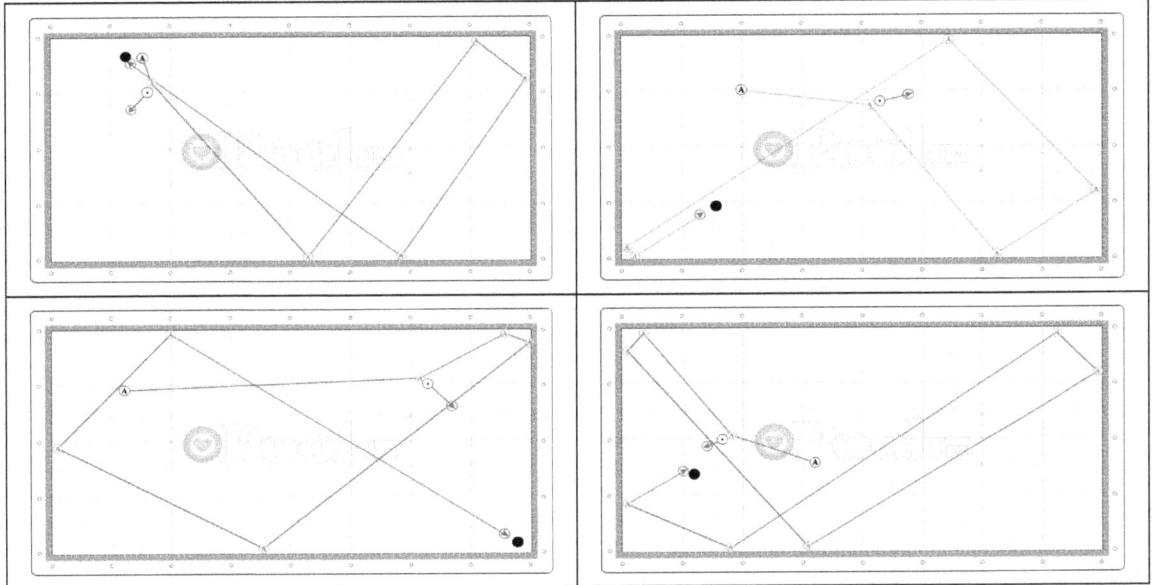

Analysis:

E:1a. _____

E:1b. _____

E:1c. _____

E:1d. _____

E:1a – Setup

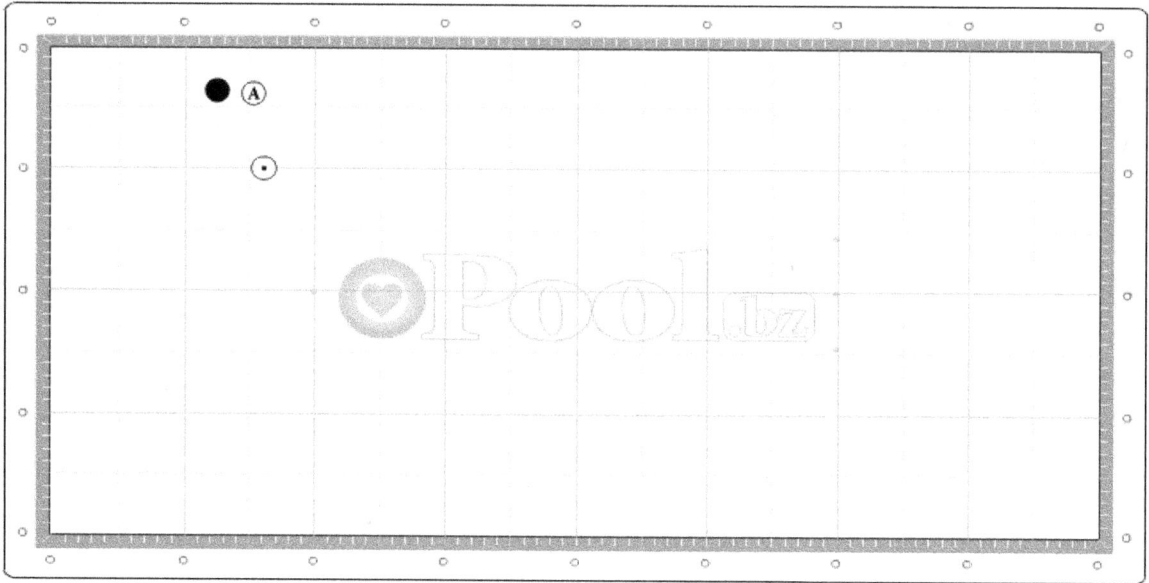

Shot Pattern

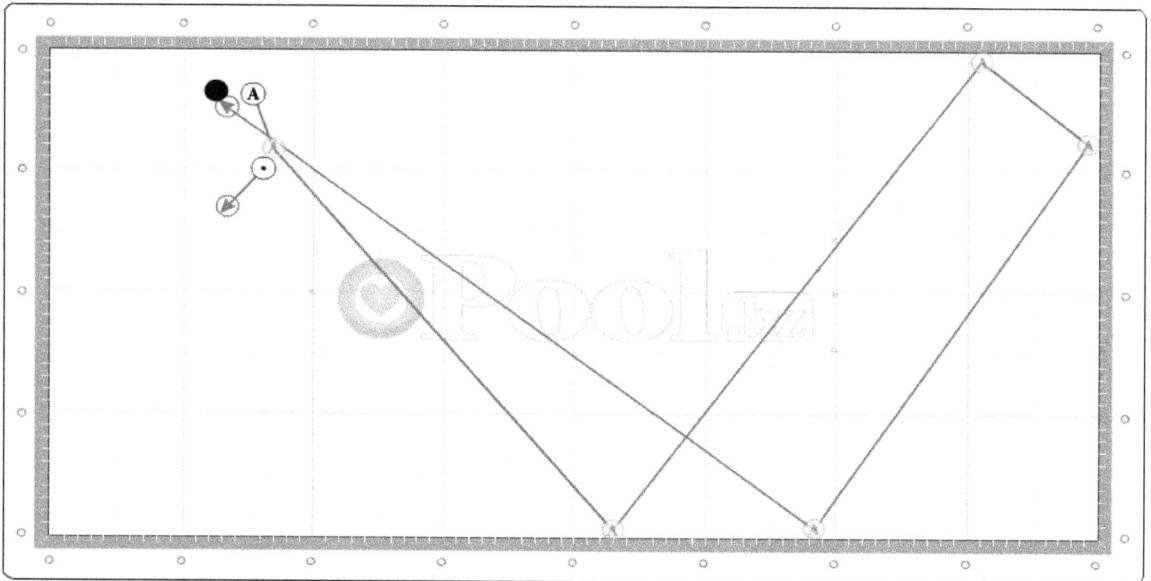

E:1b – Setup

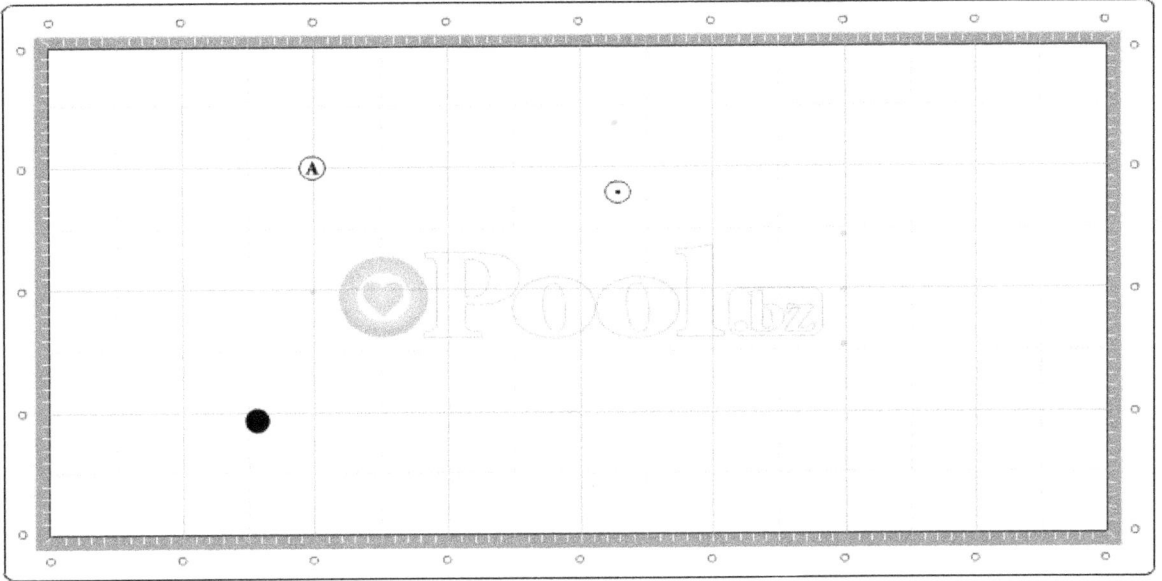

Shot Pattern

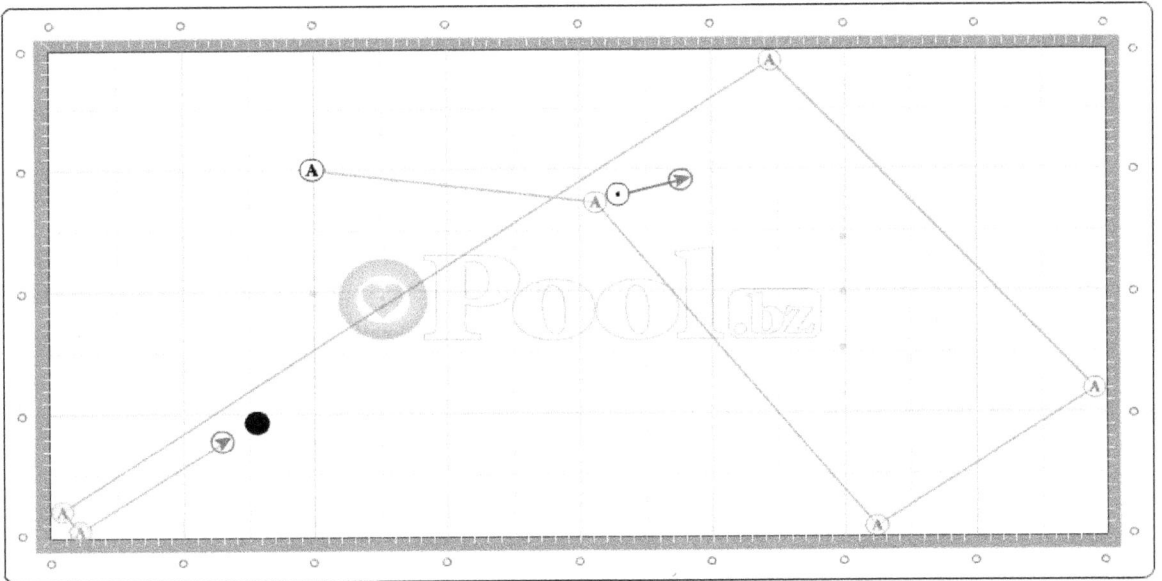

E:1c – Setup

Shot Pattern

E:1d – Setup

Shot Pattern

E: Group 2

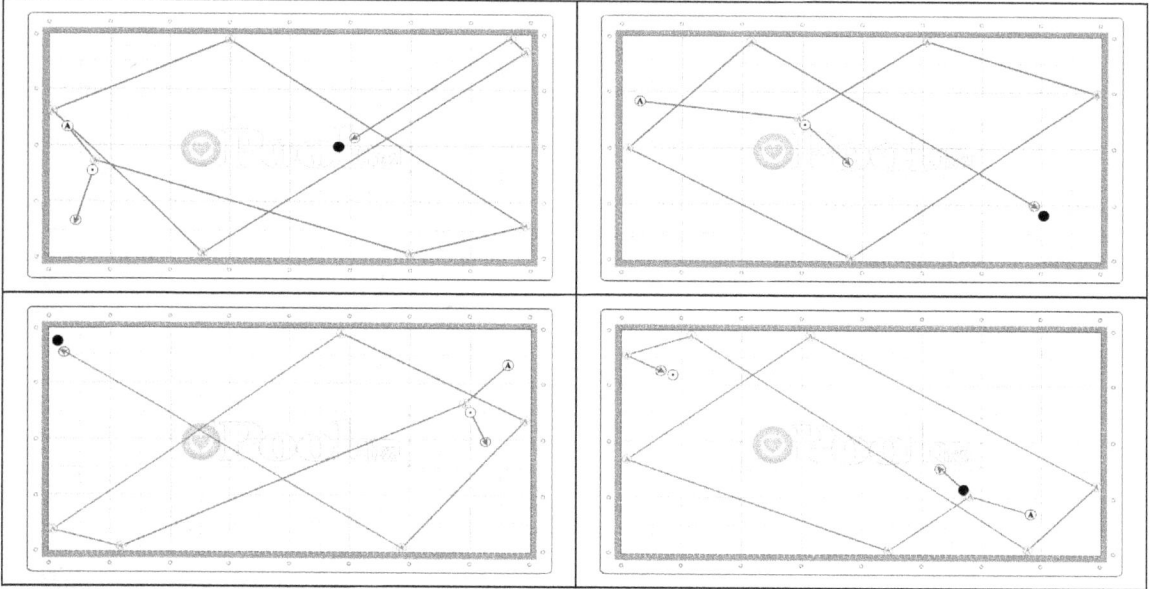

Analysis:

E:2a. _____

E:2b. _____

E:2c. _____

E:2d. _____

E:2a – Setup

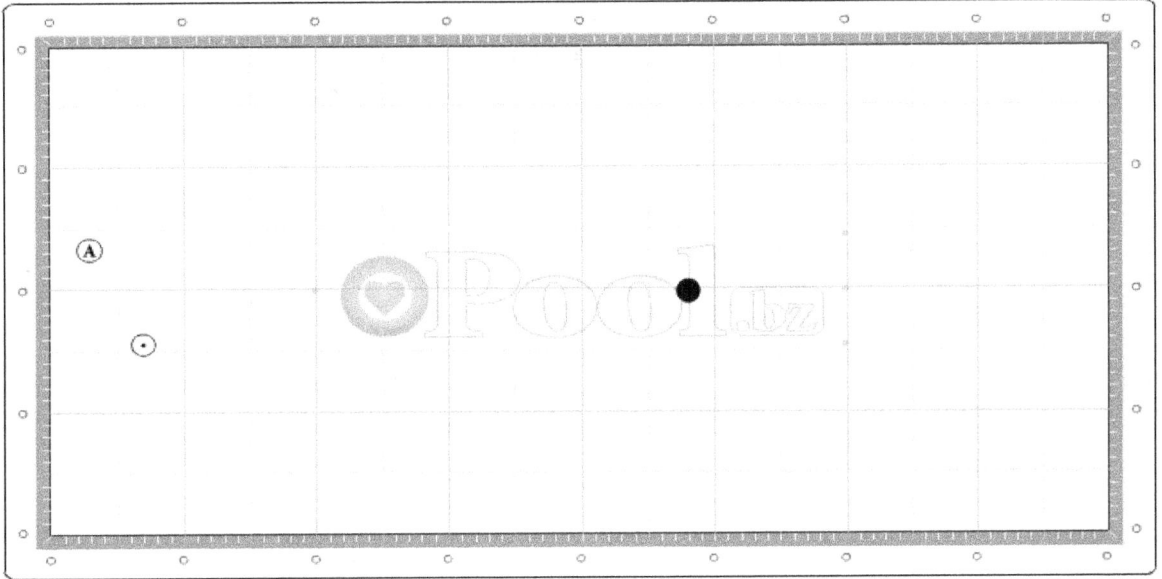

Shot Pattern

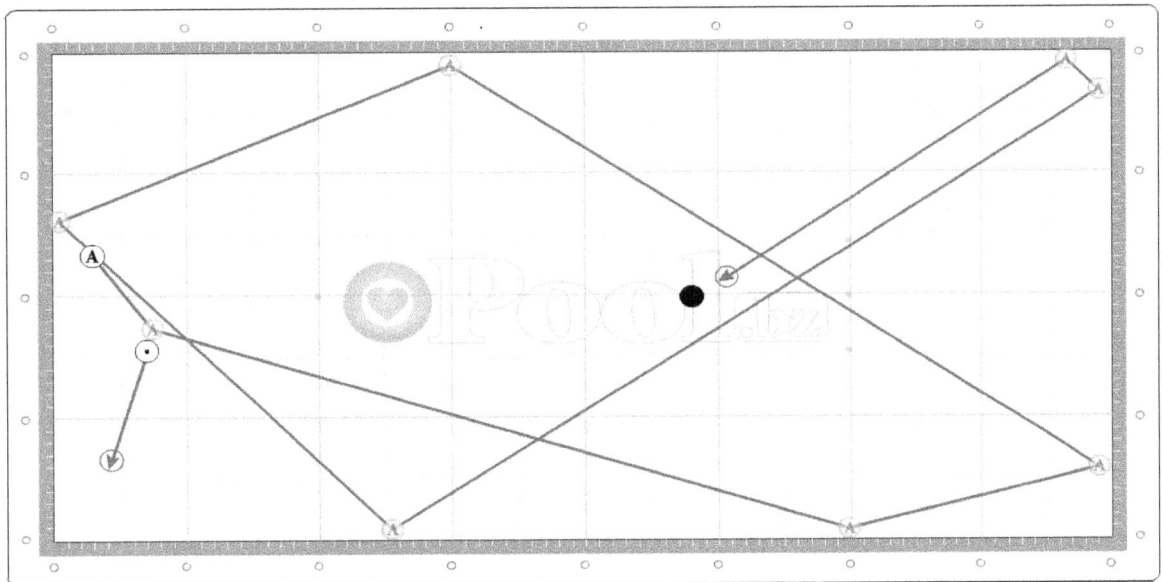

E:2b – Setup

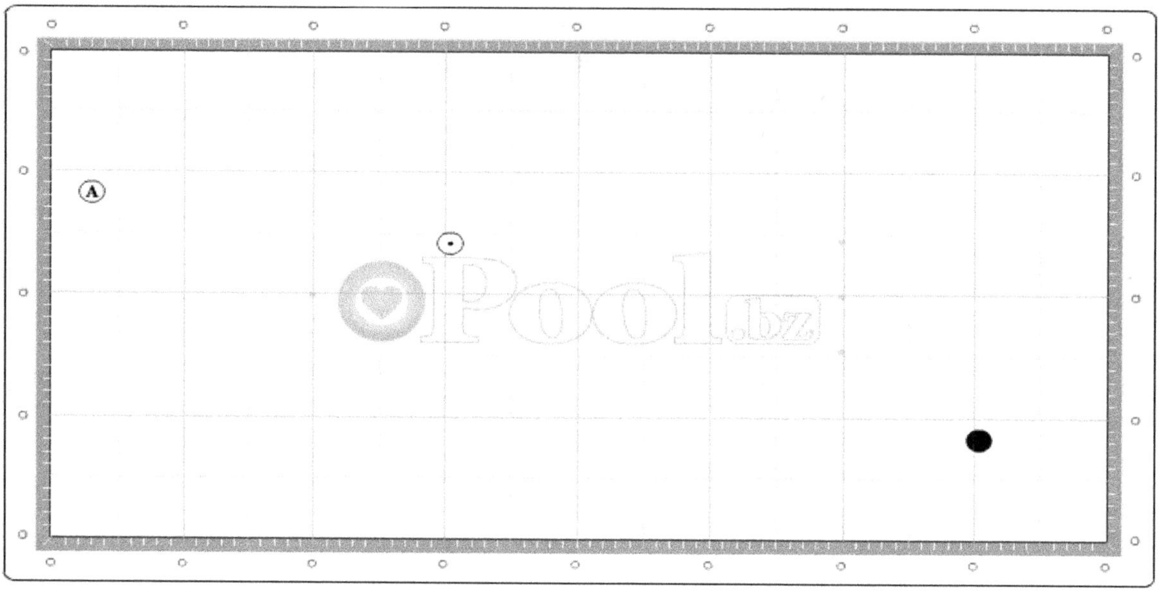

Shot Pattern

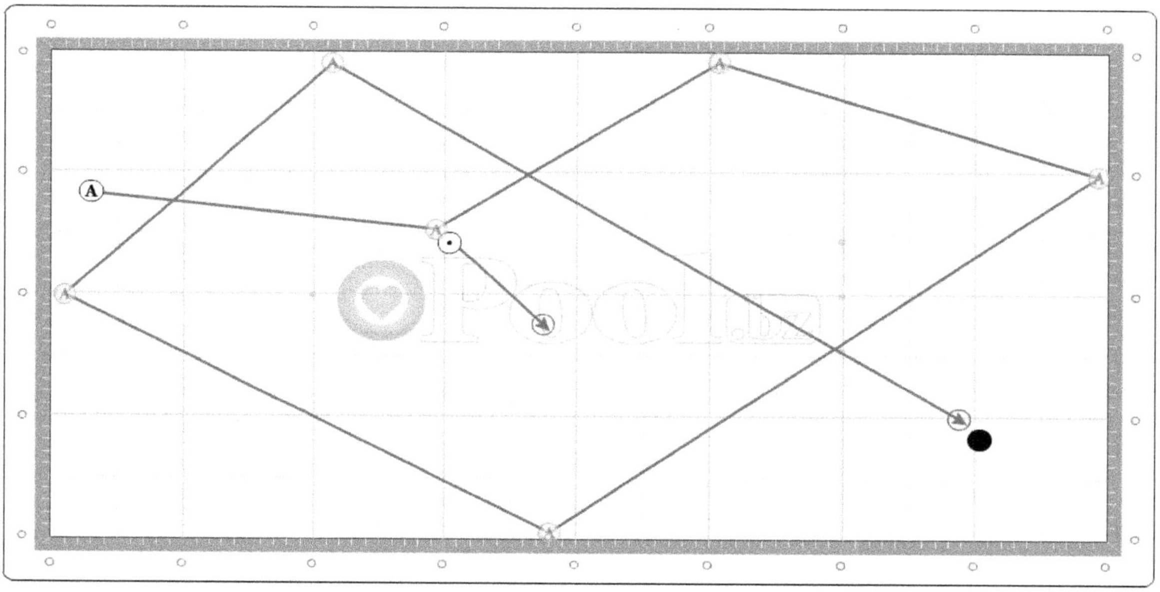

E:2c – Setup

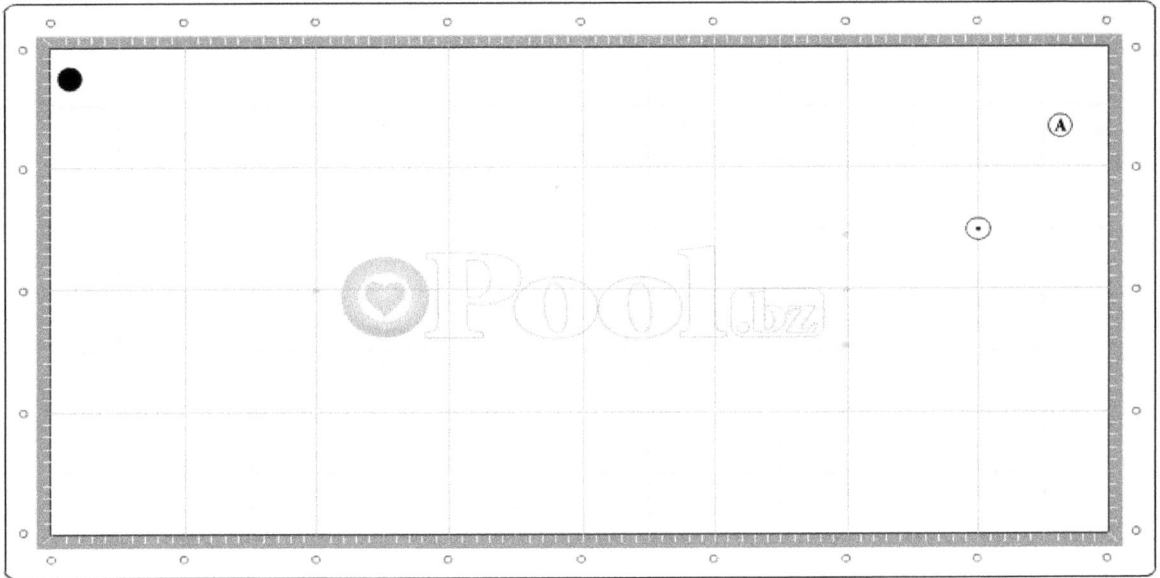

Shot Pattern

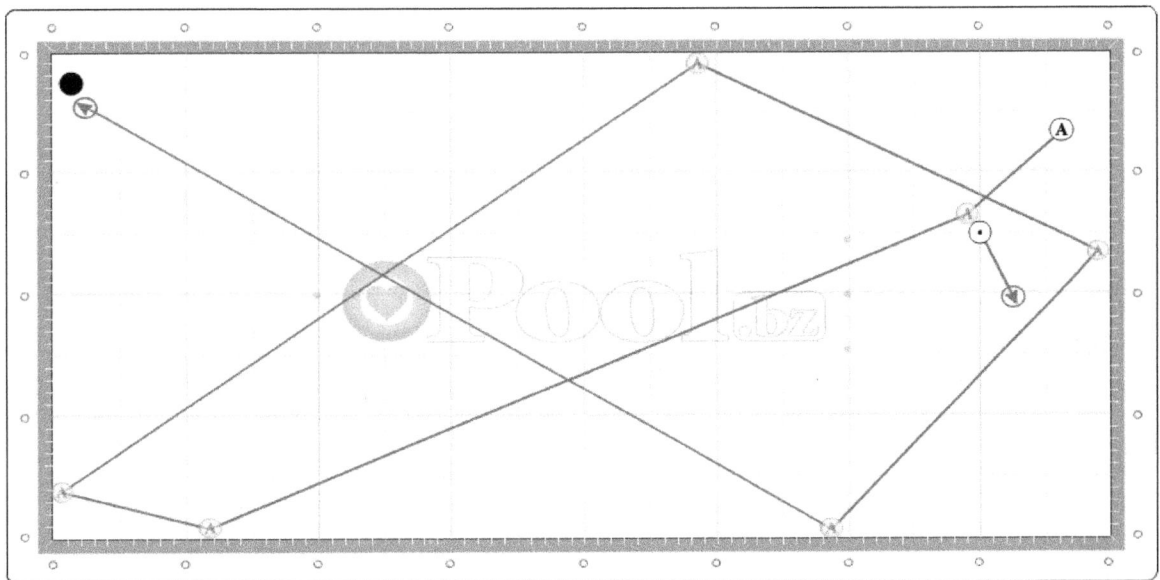

E:2d – Setup

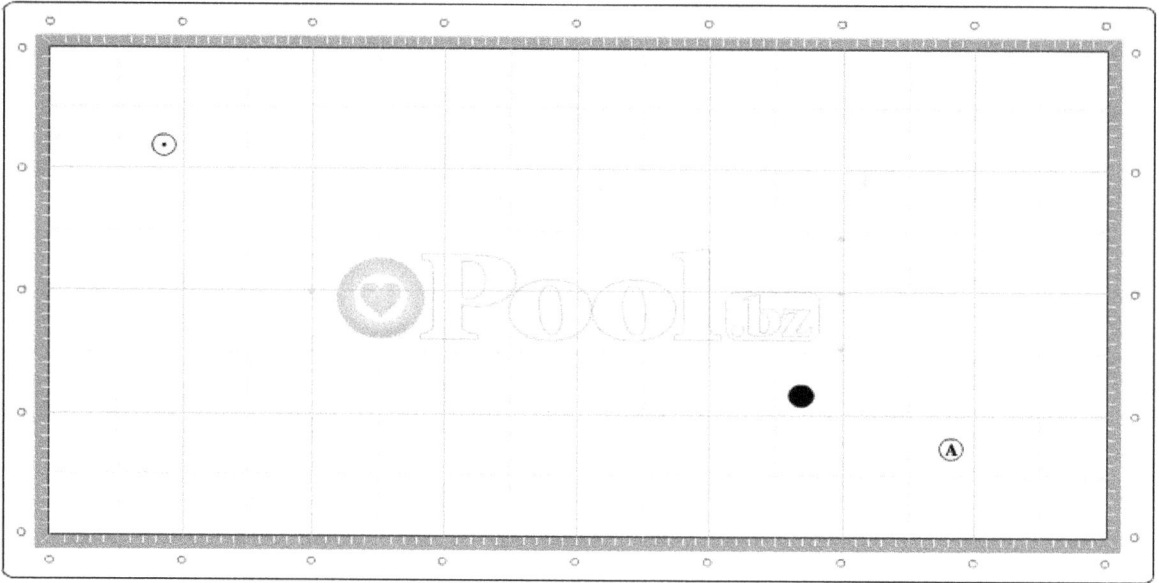

Shot Pattern

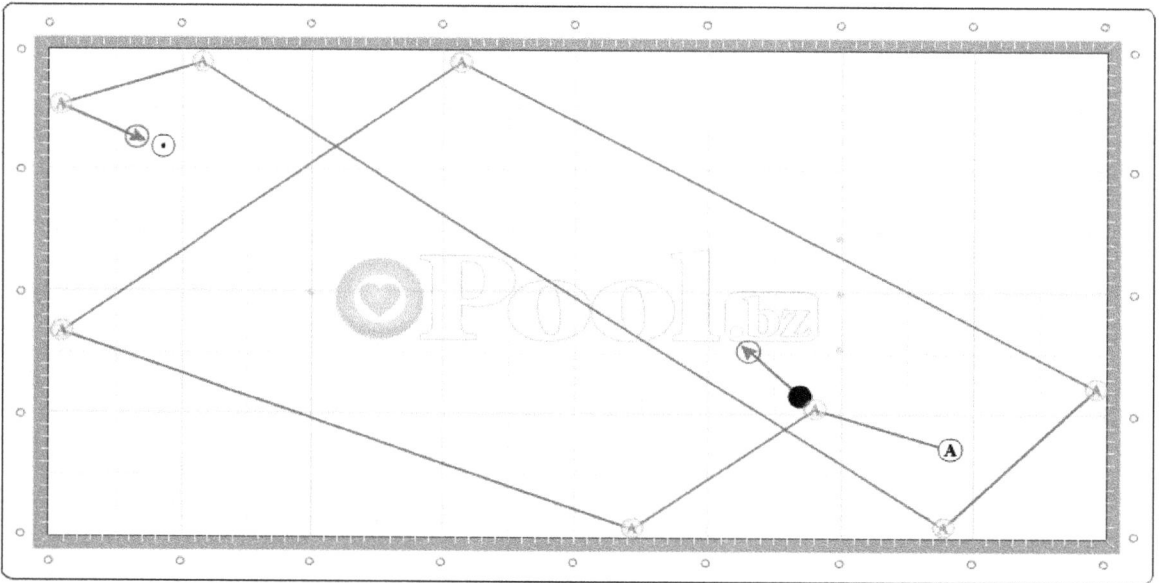

F: Fun Patterns

These shots required some imagination to see the pattern. The results were successful.

F: Group 1

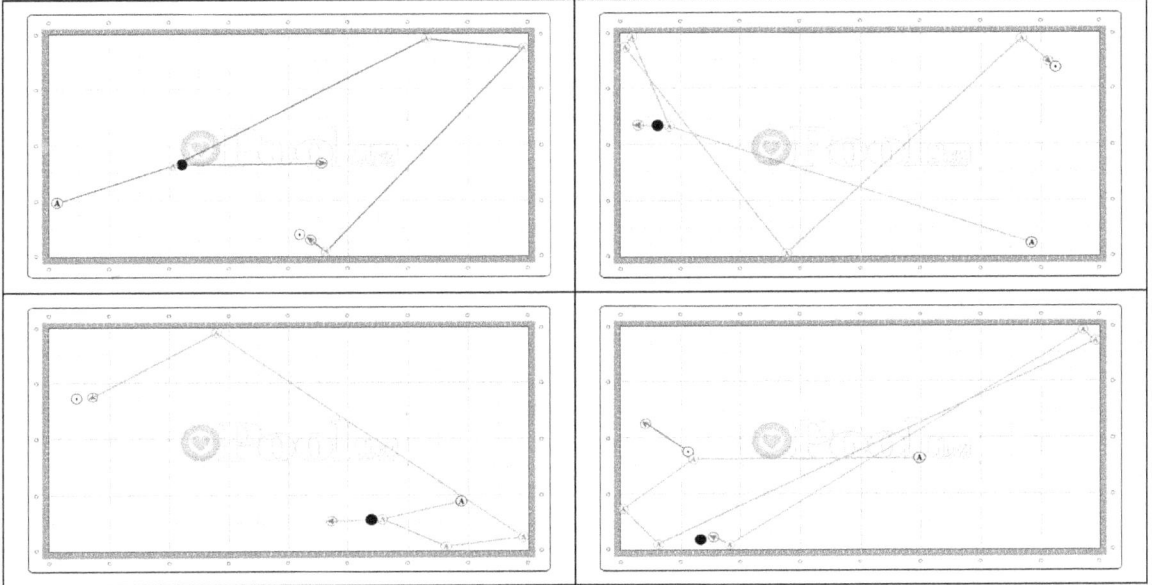

Analysis:

F:1a. _____

F:1b. _____

F:1c. _____

F:1d. _____

F:1a – Setup

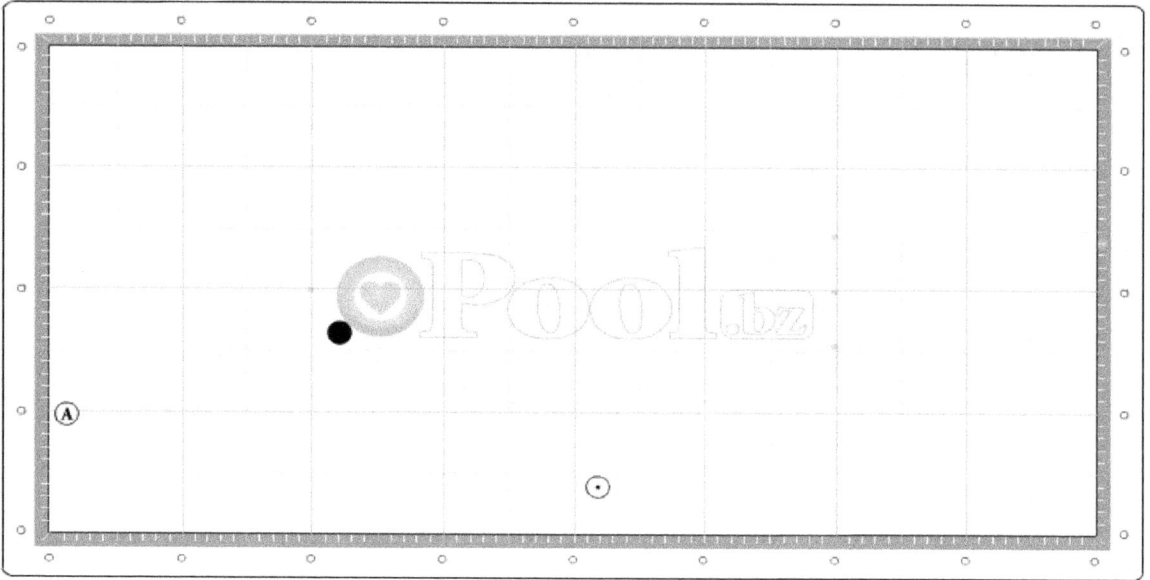

Shot Pattern

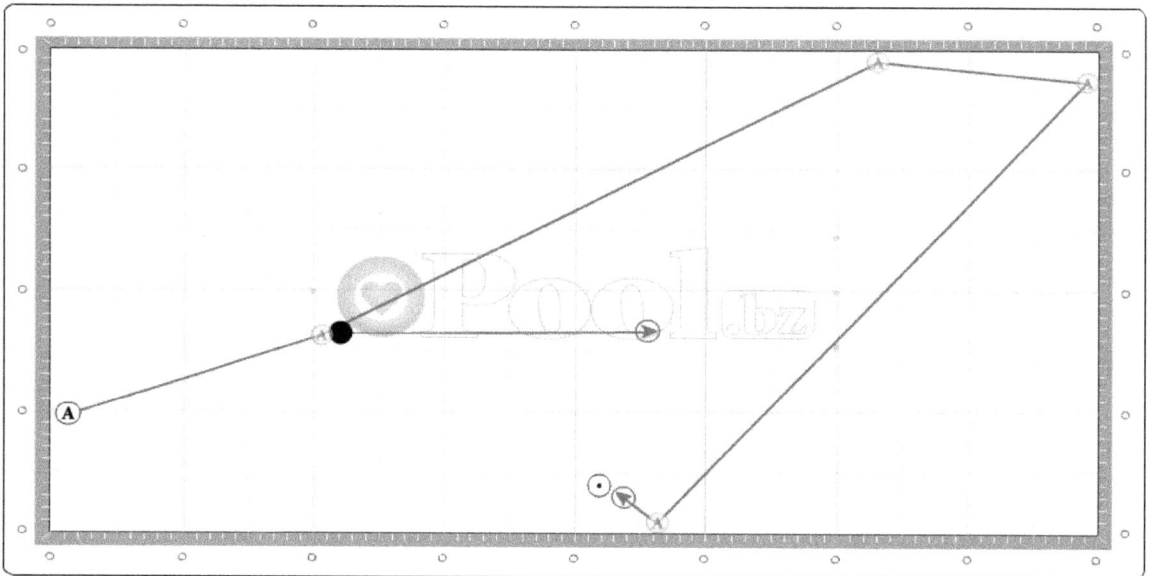

F:1b – Setup

Shot Pattern

F:1c – Setup

Shot Pattern

F:1d – Setup

Shot Pattern

F: Group 2

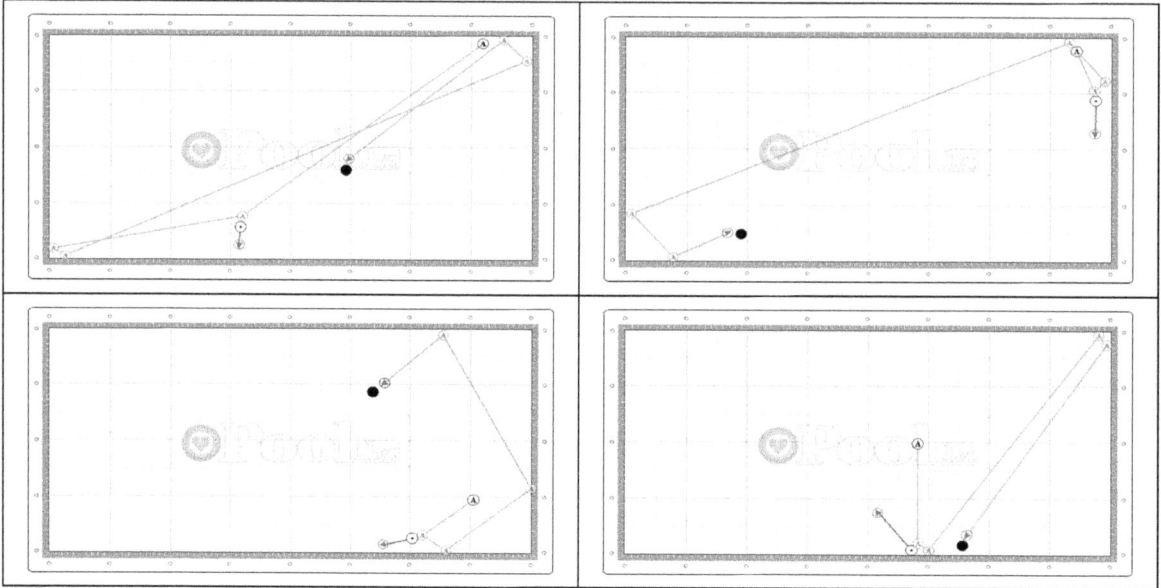

Analysis:

F:2a. _____

F:2b. _____

F:2c. _____

F:2d. _____

F:2a – Setup

Shot Pattern

F:2b – Setup

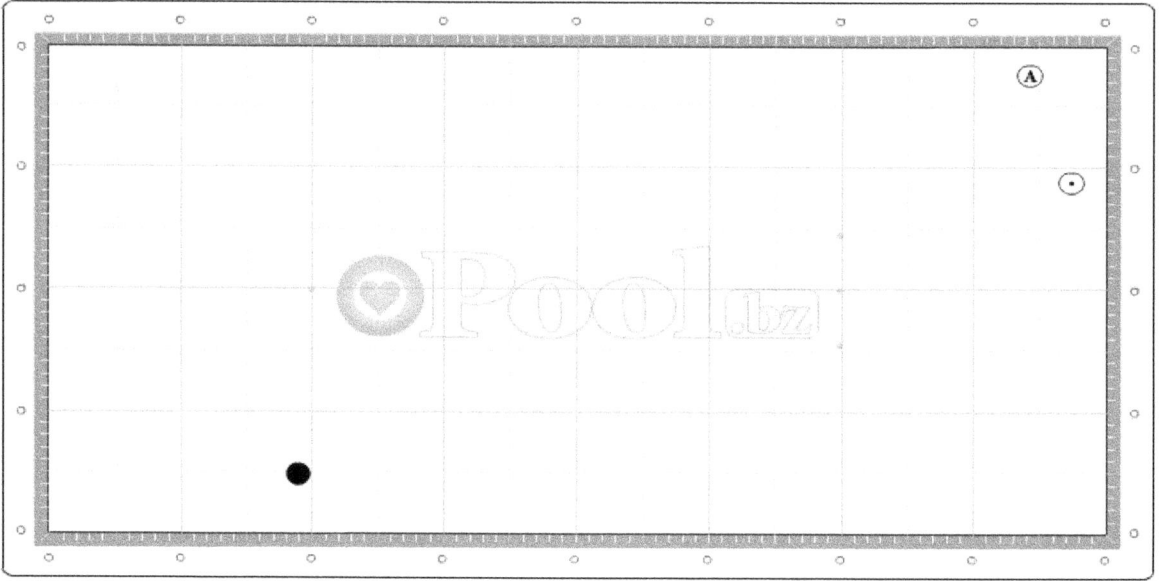

Shot Pattern

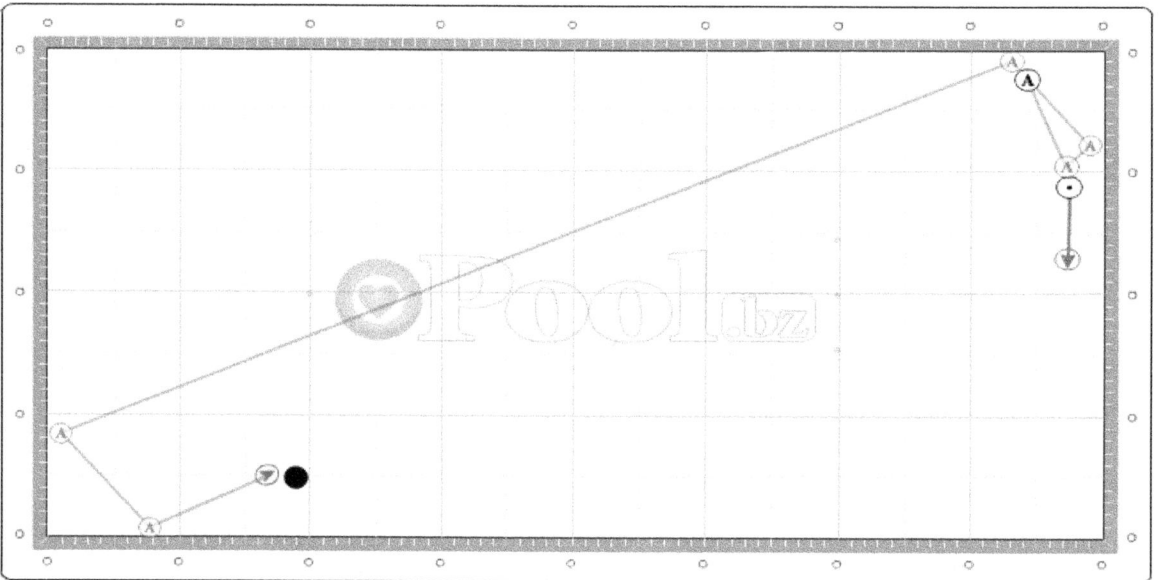

F:2c – Setup

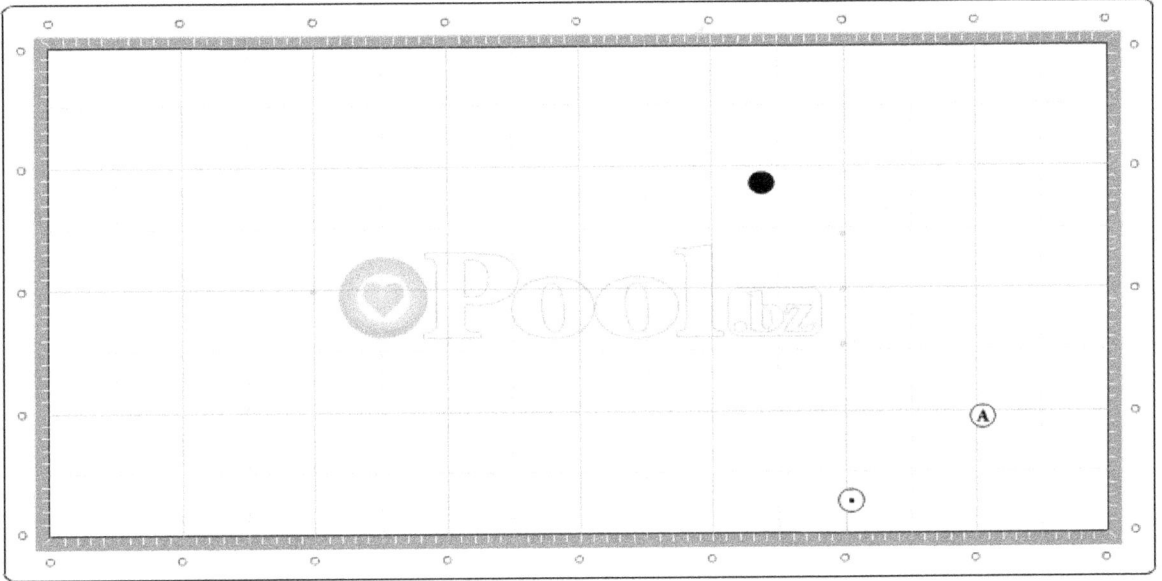

Shot Pattern

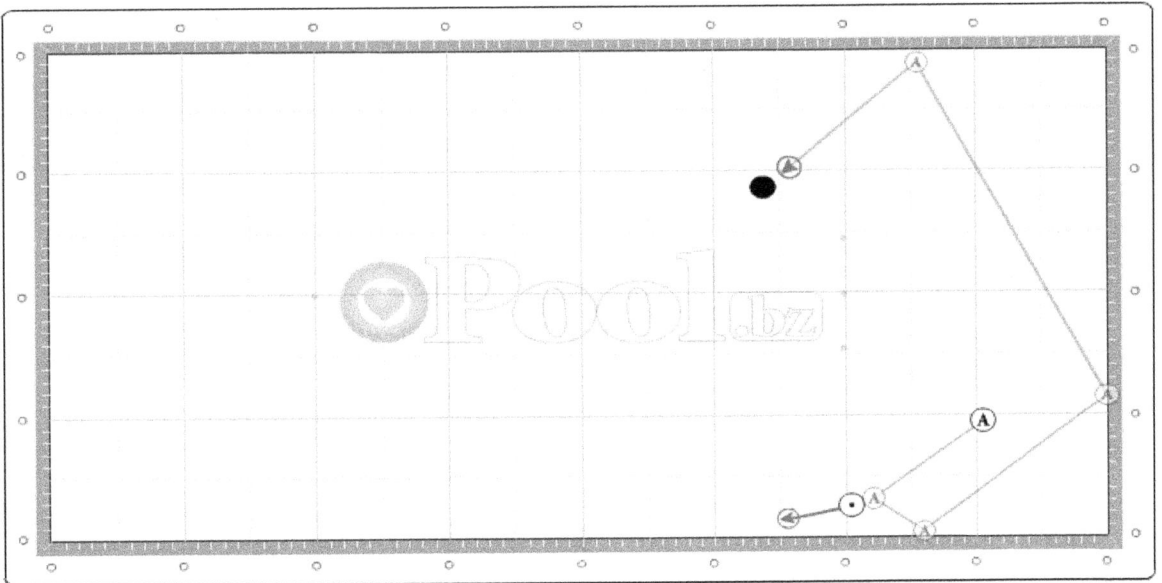

F:2d – Setup

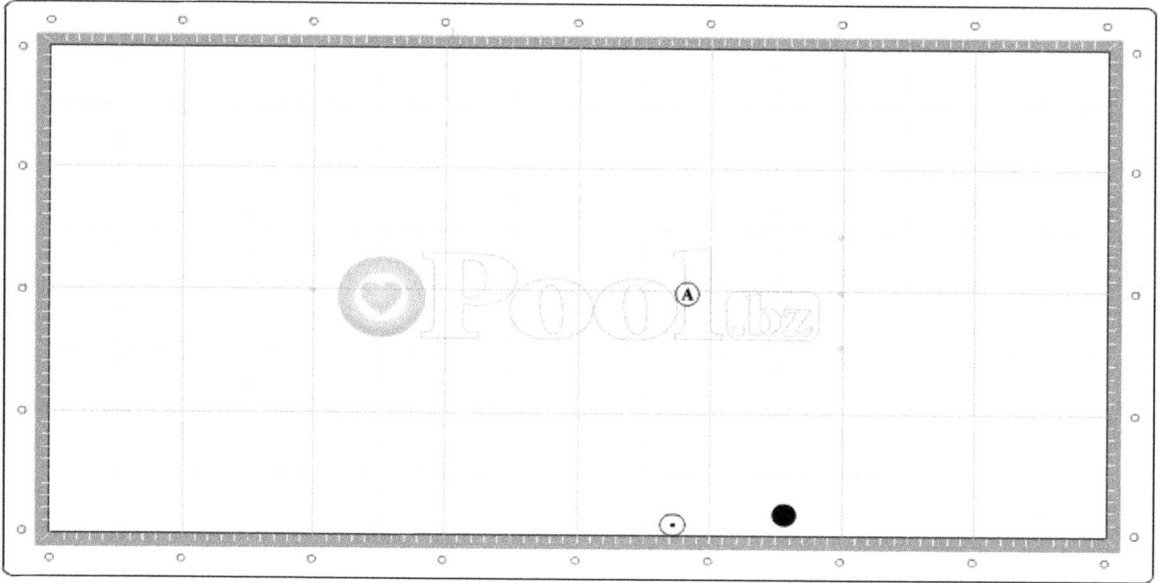

Shot Pattern

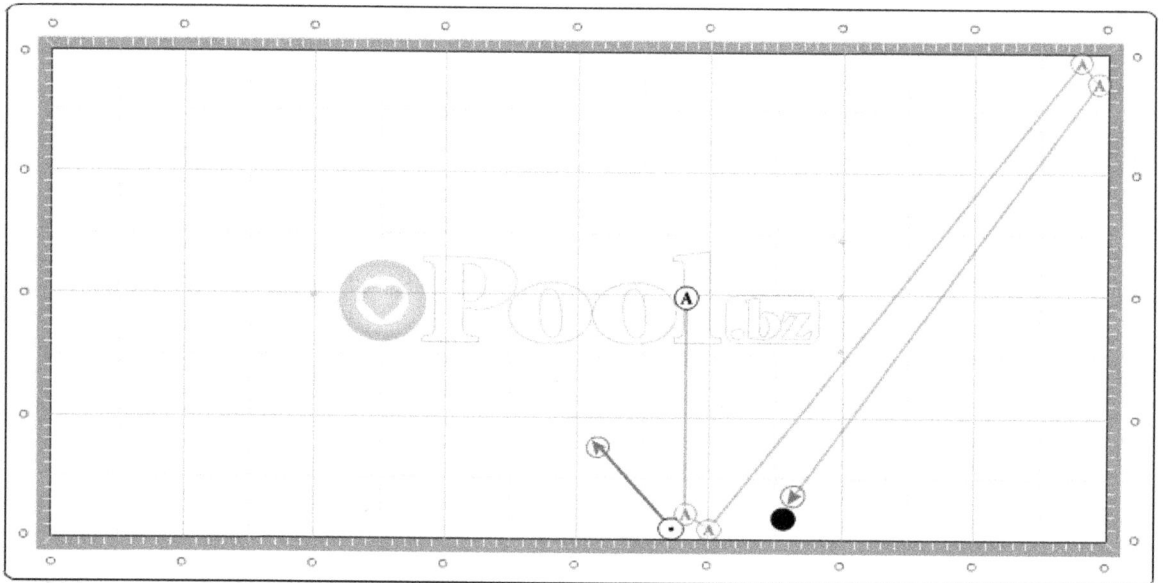

www.ingramcontent.com/pod-product-compliance
Lightning Source LLC
Chambersburg PA
CBHW080600090426
42735CB00016B/3299